Discovering Stand-up Paddleboarding

Progressive SUP From Cruise to Downwind, Surf, Race, Foil, Yoga, Workout, Fishing

Milokai Island

© Copyright 2023 - All rights reserved.

The content contained within this book may not be reproduced, duplicated or transmitted without direct written permission from the author or the publisher.

Under no circumstances will any blame or legal responsibility be held against the publisher, or author, for any damages, reparation, or monetary loss due to the information contained within this book, either directly or indirectly.

Legal Notice:

This book is copyright protected. It is only for personal use. You cannot amend, distribute, sell, use, quote or paraphrase any part, or the content within this book, without the consent of the author or publisher.

Disclaimer Notice:

Please note the information contained within this document is for educational and entertainment purposes only. All effort has been executed to present accurate, up to date, reliable, complete information. No warranties of any kind are declared or implied. Readers acknowledge that the author is not engaged in the rendering of legal, financial, medical or professional advice. The content within this book has been derived from various sources. Please consult a licensed professional before attempting any techniques outlined in this book.

By reading this document, the reader agrees that under no circumstances is the author responsible for any losses, direct or indirect, that are incurred as a result of the use of the information contained within this document, including, but not limited to, errors, omissions, or inaccuracies.

Table of Contents

Contents

Table of Contents 3
Introduction 9
   The Start 9
   The Good 10
   The Next Step 11
Chapter 1: Where to Go 12
   Lakes 12
      Features 12
      Tips 13
   Rivers 14
      Features 14
      Tips 15
   Oceans 16
      Features 16
      Tips 17
   Canals and Swamps 18
      Features 18
      Tips 19
   Yes, You Can Also Go Fishing 21
      SUP Anglers: What Are They? 22
      Fishing Tips 22
   Fun Fact 24
Chapter 2: Equipment 25
   SUP Boards 25

Fun Fact..27
  Inflatable or regular SUP board? 27
  Inflatable SUP board: 27
  Regular SUP hard board: 28
  Material and Repair 29
  Fins: Fin Placement and Fin Box 30
  Rail Guard 33
  Surface 33
  Paddle 34
  Leash 36
  Carrier 37
Fun Fact..37
Chapter 3: Gear, Safety Measures and Basic Skills........... 38
  Gear 38
    Life Jacket or Vest... 39
    Impact Vest 40
    Helmet... 40
  Other Useful Items.. 42
    Waterproof Watch 42
    Waterproof Sunglasses 43
    Portable Shower 44
    Waterproof Bag 45
    Leggings 46
    Hooded Changing Towel or Poncho.......................47
    Electric Pump.. 48
    Surf Wax... 49
  Super Basic Skills 50
  Fun Fact..51

Chapter 4: Speed - Downwind, Race, and Rapids (Whitewater) 52

Downwind 52
- How to Downwind 53
- Top Five Unforgettable Downwind Races in History 55

Race 56
- Racing 57
- Participating in a SUP Race 59
- Tips 60

Paddle Through Rapids in the River 61
- Inspiration 62

Fun Fact 63

Chapter 5: Surfing 64

Surfing 101 64
- Reasons to Surf 64
- Gear up! 65
- Surf Stance 65
- Quick Turn 67
- Paddle Out 67
- Paddle into a Wave 68
- How to Catch a Wave 70

Surfing Etiquette 71
- Rules of the Water 71
- Right-of-Way Rules 72
- Advanced SUP Surfing 73
- Advanced Techniques 74
- Basic Etiquette Tips for Beginners 75
- Etiquette in Crowded Surf Spots 76

Forecasts, Tides and Conditions 77
- Surf Forecasts 77
- Tides 78
- Surfing Conditions 79

Fun Fact 80

Chapter 6: SUP Foil 81

What Is Foiling? 81

The Experience of Foiling 82

Foiling Techniques 82
- Pumping 83
- Carving 84
- Downwind Foiling 86

Fun Fact 87

Foiling and Its Challenges 87

Benefits of Foiling 89

Thoughts from the Surfing Community 90
- A Negative Outlook 90
- Positive Vibes 90
- The Impact of Foiling on the SUP Community 91

The New Normal: Surfers, Paddlers, and Foilers Sharing the Lineup 92

The Future Looks Bright 93

Chapter 7: SUP Yoga and Workout 95

How Many Calories Can You Burn? 95

Benefits of SUP Yoga and Workout 96

Getting Started With SUP Yoga and Workout 97
- Helpful Item 97
- Location: A Safe and Calm Space 97

- Tips (Especially for Beginners) 98
- SUP Yoga Poses 99
  - Basic Poses 99
  - Intermediate Poses 101
  - Advanced Poses 102
- SUP Yoga Sequence 104
- SUP Workout 105
  - SUP Workout Routine 106
  - Cool Down and Stretching Exercises 107
  - Modifying for Different Fitness Levels 108
- SUP Yoga and Workout Classes and Retreats 109
  - What to Expect 109
  - Recommendations 110
  - SUP in Retirement Homes 111
- Fun Fact 112

Chapter 8: Travel Tips 113
- The Benefits of Traveling With a SUP Board 113
- Fun Fact 114
- Research Your Destination 115
  - Checking Regulations and Restrictions 115
  - Finding the Best SUP Spots 116
  - Learning Local Weather and Water Conditions 118
- Travel with your board 119
  - Choosing an Inflatable Board 120
  - Protecting Your Board and Paddle 121
  - A Board Bag 121
  - Proper Packing 123
- Renting vs. Buying 124

- Why Rent? 124
- Getting Rid of the Hassle 125
- Dressing Appropriately 125
- Using Wetsuits and Rash Guards 126
- The Usefulness of a PFD 126
- Knowing Your Limits 127
- Avoiding Unnecessary Risks 128
- Conclusion 130
- References 134

Introduction

Do you remember the last time you truly felt alive and connected to nature?

The wind in your hair, the sun on your face, the sound of waves crashing against the shore?

For me, that feeling comes every time I paddle out on my stand-up paddleboard and immerse myself in the beauty of Hawaii's waters.

I am Kai of Milokai Island, and I have been fortunate enough to make SUP my passion and my lifestyle.

The Start

It all started when I accidentally caught a wave while stand-up paddleboarding in Hawaii. Flipped over by the wave's power, I looked up and saw an incredible view of the shoreline that was a quarter mile away.

The waves were crashing, sea turtles were swimming around, and surfers and paddlers were enjoying the waves.

I felt amazing when catching the wave and felt so good in the water. It was the moment I was hooked by being in the water.

I decided to take the journey of learning stand-up paddleboarding, or SUP. I researched everything I could about the water sport and bought my first SUP board.

At first, I struggled to stand on it and paddle to move forward, especially since the board was relatively small for beginners. All the trials and errors with a SUP board continued, and it became my weekend routine for a while.

Eventually, it took me to where I was able to enjoy riding bumps in the river with strong winds, going over crashing whitewater, and catching green waves in the ocean, which was the view burned into my head.

The Good

From then on, I realized I couldn't be more passionate about SUP. Just the thought of it alone makes me smile.

One of the best things about SUP is that it's a low-impact activity, which means it's easier on your joints than high-impact activities like running. According to Burns (2022), you can burn up to 500 calories an hour while paddling.

The best part? You don't even realize you're exercising because you're too busy having fun on the water.

Plus, the benefits of SUP aren't just about physical fitness. SUP sessions are also amazing ways of connecting with nature.

There's something incredibly calming and peaceful about being out on the water—surrounded by nothing but the sound of the waves or the beauty of your environment. As you're standing up on the board, you get a unique perspective and a chance to see things from a different point of view.

I want to help others find the same passion and joy that I found in SUP.

As an experienced SUP enthusiast, I know firsthand how challenging it can be to get started and improve your skills. I've lived in different places by the Pacific Ocean and the Atlantic Ocean and traveled to different valleys, rivers, and lakes in the US, Australia, Asia, and Mexico to pursue my passion for SUP.

Through all of my experiences, I have gained a deep understanding of the problems and pains that many people face when they start SUP, such as struggling to balance on the board, not knowing how to paddle properly, or feeling intimidated by more experienced riders.

I've been there myself, and I know how discouraging it can be.

That's what this book is for.

Like with any book about SUP, the idea is to provide you with guidance through your journey. It doesn't matter if you're a complete beginner or an experienced paddler. As long as you want to explore your SUP options, this book is for you.

In the next pages, you'll find everything you need to know to get started with SUP. This includes the basics of how to select a location where you want to go for SUP, choose the right equipment, and basic knowledge on different types of SUP.

The Next Step

This book isn't just a beginner's guide.

It's also a resource for more experienced paddlers who want to explore more SUP options.

Here, I will introduce recent trends, go-to options in the sport, basic tips for different SUP, and more. All of which will help you stay up-to-date with the latest equipment and methods.

I know that many people are hesitant to try SUP because they think it's too difficult or they don't have the right skills.

However, I firmly believe that anyone can do it if they want to. You don't have to be an athlete or an expert in water sports to enjoy many benefits of SUP.

So what are you waiting for?

Chapter 1: Where to Go

Welcome to the world of stand-up paddleboarding!

New to this water sport?

Then you're probably wondering about the best places to try it out.

The good news is that SUP is a versatile activity. Almost everybody can enjoy it, and on many bodies of water—lakes, rivers, the ocean with gigantic waves, you name it.

So let's explore your options.

In this chapter, we'll explore different types of water bodies and environments where you can go paddleboarding or take your skills to the next level.

We'll also cover SUP fishing—yes, there's such a thing! We'll discuss what makes it different from fishing on a kayak, SUP fishing tips, and more.

Lakes

SUP is popular on lakes because lakes have calm and flat waters, which are great for beginners or those who want a relaxing paddle.

Lakes are also often surrounded by beautiful scenery, making them a perfect place for nature lovers. Great lakes to check out are Lake George (New York), Lake Norman (North Carolina), and Lake Waikiki (Hawaii).

Features

According to studies, the water in lakes is typically deep enough to prevent you from hitting the bottom when you fall off the board, and you don't have to worry about sharks or other ocean predators. (Regan, 2021). This makes it a great venue for beginners to learn and practice the sport.

However, do note that lakes often lack the vigilant supervision of lifeguards. Without lifeguards, you need to take safety precautions seriously and not assume anything.

Here's what makes lakes fascinating:

- **Calm waters:** Due to their calm waters, lakes are an excellent place for beginners to learn the basics of SUP. The still water allows for better balance and less resistance, making it easier to get the hang of paddling and maneuvering the board.
- **Variety of activities:** Lakes offer a variety of activities for SUP enthusiasts, including fishing, camping, hiking, and picnicking. With so many activities to choose from, you can easily make a day or weekend trip out of your SUP adventure.
- **Less crowded:** Unlike busy rivers and oceans, lakes are often less crowded, providing a more peaceful and relaxing environment for SUP enthusiasts. With fewer boats and other watercraft around, you'll have more room to paddle and explore.

Tips

Lakes are where you can find enthusiasts of other water sports, like kayaking, canoeing, and water skiing. As such, they present an opportunity for SUP enthusiasts to mingle and make friends with those who also love water activities.

How to make the most out of SUP on a lake.

- **Choose a calm and clear day to paddle:** Paddling on a calm and clear day can ensure a safer and more enjoyable SUP experience, as windy and rough conditions can make it difficult to maintain balance on the board.

- **Watch out for boats and jet skis:** There may be other watercraft in the area. Give them enough space so you can prevent collisions and other accidents.

- **Stay near the shoreline but stay away from shallow water:** Staying near the shoreline can provide a safer and more stable environment for paddling. If you paddle out too far from the shore, you may have trouble coming back to the shore due to strong winds or something unexpected. If you want to paddle out far, just know your limits.

Also, stay away from shallow water to minimize the risk of falling off rocks or reef bottoms, or getting hit by something sharp or unexpected on the bottom.

Rivers

SUP on rivers can offer a more challenging experience for those looking for an adrenaline rush. Rivers can have varying currents and obstacles, making a SUP session on a river a fun way to test one's balance and skills.

Plus, many rivers are located in scenic areas and offer a unique perspective of the surrounding landscapes.

Features

Paddling on a river can be a thrilling experience—as the water conditions can vary depending on the season and geographical location. The wind, water from the mountains, steepness and shape of the land can all impact the water conditions.

You can adjust your paddleboarding style based on where you choose to paddle, as different parts of the river can provide unique conditions.

Why are rivers so great?

- **Strong currents:** Rivers have strong currents that can add an extra challenge to your SUP adventure. Understanding the direction and speed of the current is crucial to navigating a river safely and effectively.

- **Rocks and boulders:** Rivers often have a rocky bottom that can be challenging to navigate, and boulders can create obstacles that require skilled maneuvering. Paddlers need to be aware of these features and have proper safety equipment to avoid injury.

- **Changing water levels:** Rivers can experience changing water levels due to factors such as rain, snowmelt, and dam releases. Paddlers need to be aware of the water levels and the potential dangers they pose.

Tips

During the summer, winds blow from the ocean to the mountainside, creating bumps in the water. Some people paddle on these bumps while the wind blows from behind, requiring different techniques than riding waves.

These conditions are specific to downwind races held in Colombia River Gorge—one of the most popular downwind destinations.

However, depending on your downwind destination, you can expect different types of water or wind conditions.

Tips for paddling in a river:

- **Watch out for rocks and obstacles in the water:** To avoid injury, look out for anything in the way. Hitting an obstacle, such as rocks, can damage your SUP board if it is not inflatable.
- **Paddle in the direction of the wind to enjoy a roller coaster ride:** Paddling in the same direction as the wind can help you paddle very fast and make your ride smoother and more enjoyable. However, remember to make arrangements to travel back to the starting point or end your downwind session without hiking back and leaving your board behind. If you try to paddle back against the wind for a long distance, it can quickly drain your energy and you can get stuck in the middle of the water.

Oceans

SUP in the ocean is a great way to explore the open waters and enjoy the waves.

Ocean paddleboarding can offer a more intense workout than paddling on lakes or rivers due to the constant motion of the waves. It's also a great way to spot marine life, such as dolphins, whales, and sea turtles.

You can choose between flatwater or waves when paddling in the ocean, and the conditions can vary greatly depending on factors such as the tide, wind, and ocean floor.

Features

The ocean is a vast and dynamic body of water that offers one-of-a-kind features and challenges for SUP enthusiasts.

Why oceans are great for SUP:

- **Waves:** According to Regan (2021), learning how to ride waves is why paddlers go to the ocean. Riding waves is fun, and while it may take a while to learn, compared to paddleboarding on flat water, it can help create a one-of-a-kind SUP session.

- **Wind:** The ocean is often windy, which can create choppy conditions that can make paddling more challenging. Understanding water conditions and how they can impact your route is important for a safe SUP experience.

- **Marine life:** The ocean is home to a wide variety of marine life, including dolphins, sea turtles, and even whales in some areas. While it's exciting to encounter these animals, it's crucial to respect their habitat and keep a safe distance.

Tips

The ocean floor can be rocky and uneven, with reefs and other underwater obstacles posing a significant danger to SUP riders. That's why it's important to understand the geography of the ocean floor or water condition of your chosen location.

So, try to paddle in an area where you feel safe. However, if you want to paddle over rocks or reefs, just make sure you take safety precautions.

How to get the most fun out of oceans:

- **Check the weather and ocean conditions before heading out:** Be vigilant and check the weather and ocean conditions before heading out for any water activity.

  This can help you avoid potentially dangerous situations such as strong winds, rough seas, stormy weather, or a large amount of box jellyfish. You can check weather warnings and ocean conditions through various sources such as local news, weather apps, or online marine forecasts.

- **Start with small waves and work your way up to larger ones:** If you're new to SUP or any other water sport, it's important to start with small waves and gradually work your way up to larger ones.

   This will help you build up your skills while reducing the risk of injury. Starting with small waves also allows you to learn the fundamentals of the sport, such as paddling, standing up, and turning, before attempting more advanced maneuvers.

- **Use a wide stance to maintain balance in choppy water:** In rough water conditions, it's advisable to use a wide stance to maintain balance on your board. It lets you distribute your weight evenly and enables greater stability. As a result, it becomes easier for you to stay in an upright position.

Canals and Swamps

An article published in *The New York Times* claims that exploring a swamp or forest on a SUP board can be an exhilarating experience (Stinchecombe, 2023). The serene waters of the swamp offer a peaceful escape from the hustle and bustle of everyday life.

Features

Canals and swamps offer still waters perfect for a relaxing paddle, and the surrounding nature can provide a peaceful environment for paddlers to enjoy.

They're also often home to a variety of wildlife, such as birds, turtles, and beavers, making them a good place for nature enthusiasts. While they may not be as popular as lakes, rivers, or oceans, they offer their own set of challenges and rewards.

Here are some features unique to canals and swamps for SUP enthusiasts to explore:

- **Narrow passages:** You need good maneuvering skills to navigate the narrow areas of canals and swamps.

    True—it presents another challenge for paddlers because it means going through tight places and distancing yourself from submerged logs and overhanging branches, but once you get better at maneuvering, the experience will be worth your while.

- **Slow currents:** Paddleboarding at these places may require more effort because of the slow-moving current. As long as you're excellent at maintaining your balance and adjusting the way you paddle, you'll be safe.

- **Murky water:** These places can make it challenging for you to see underwater as they may have stained or murky water.

Tips

A paddleboard allows you to navigate shallow waters that are inaccessible by boat or kayak. You can paddle through the narrow passages of the swamp, surrounded by towering trees, lush greenery, and the sounds of nature.

However, take safety precautions. Always check the water conditions, and be mindful of obstacles such as logs or branches that may be lurking beneath the water's surface.

It's also wise to bring along insect repellent and wear protective clothing to prevent bug bites and scratches from vegetation.

Below are tricks to help you have the best time on canals and swamps.

- **Wear bug spray and sun protection:** When spending time outdoors, it's important to protect yourself from sunburn and insect bites. Applying bug spray and wearing sunscreen, hats, and protective clothing can help prevent discomfort, irritation, and potential health risks.

- **Watch out for underwater obstacles like logs and rocks:** Just like when swimming or boating in natural bodies of water, it's important to keep an eye out for potential underwater hazards like logs, rocks, or other obstacles that could cause injury or damage to your board. Be sure to stay alert and follow any posted signs or warnings.

- **Stay on waterways and follow posted regulations:** Designated waterways and posted guidelines exist for a reason: to ensure your safety. Staying on marked waterways and following regulations also help you show respect for the rights of the property owners.

Yes, You Can Also Go Fishing

Paddleboard fishing is a relatively new and exciting way to fish. It has gained a lot of popularity in recent years because it's a rad way to enjoy the outdoors, get some exercise, and catch some fish all at the same time.

One of its perks? The ability to access otherwise inaccessible areas.

With a paddleboard, anglers can easily maneuver through shallow or rocky waters that would be challenging to navigate with a traditional boat. This allows them to reach areas where fish tend to congregate, increasing their chances of a successful catch.

Another advantage of paddleboard fishing is its portability.

Paddleboards are lightweight and easy to transport, making them great for anglers who like to explore different fishing locations. You can also load them onto a car roof rack or transport them in the trunk of a car.

According to an article featured on GILI Sports, when it comes to fishing on a SUP board, understanding the tide and its impact on fish behavior can be a big deal (McCaw, 2022).

Fish are known to be more active during periods of high tide or when there is an increase in water movement.

This is because the movement of water brings with it a variety of food sources, such as small baitfish, crustaceans, and other organisms that make up the base of the aquatic food chain.

During the high tide, water levels rise and bring more water into estuaries and other fishing spots, creating more cover and structure for fish to forage and hunt.

As a result, fishing during high tide can be incredibly productive, as fish are more active and are feeding aggressively. On the other hand, during low tide, the water levels recede, exposing more of the shoreline and making it harder for fish to find cover and food.

SUP Anglers: What Are They?

SUP anglers are individuals who combine the sport of SUP with the hobby of fishing. Some of them can be windsurfers or kite surfers who go fishing while waiting for the wind to pick up.

SUP anglers use their paddleboards to access remote or hard-to-reach fishing spots that are not easily accessible by boat or on foot. The SUP board provides a stable platform for casting and reeling in fish, allowing anglers to get closer to the action and have a more immersive fishing experience.

SUP fishing has become increasingly popular in recent years as more and more people discover the benefits of combining the two outdoor activities into one. SUP fishing in the ocean, particularly, became a favorite. When there are no waves and wind, paddlers go fishing on their boards to spend time there.

Apart from being a cool activity, SUP fishing provides a one-of-a-kind perspective on what it's like to be on the water. It also allows anglers to breathe in the natural beauty of their environment. And to top it off, it's an incredible way of escaping crowded areas and the noise of traditional fishing places.

Remember to play it safe and take safety precautions. For example, wear a life jacket and use proper paddling techniques.

Fishing Tips

To engage in SUP fishing, anglers need a SUP board, a paddle, and appropriate fishing gear, such as rods, reels, and lures. They also need to ensure that their SUP board has sufficient stability and carrying capacity to accommodate their gear and any fish they may catch.

How can you make fishing on a paddleboard more exciting?

- **Go for night fishing:** Fishing on a SUP board can be a mesmerizing experience, especially at night. According to Nuttall (2022), one of its advantages is it can help you catch fish in a stealth-like manner.

  A pro tip is to bring a reliable headlamp or waterproof flashlight and practice safety measures.

- **Use polarized sunglasses:** Polarized sunglasses can be a game-changer for SUP anglers, as they help reduce glare and make it easier to spot fish and underwater structures. Polarized sunglasses can help SUP anglers see clearly into the water and increase their chances of spotting fish.

- **Bring a fish finder:** A fish finder can be a useful tool for SUP anglers who want to locate fish and underwater structures. It uses sonar technology to detect fish and can help anglers save time and effort by directing them to the most productive fishing spots.

- **Try fly fishing:** SUP fly fishing can be a fun and challenging way to catch fish. With its relatively small casting range and specialized gear, fly fishing requires more skill and precision than traditional spin fishing.

  However, the technique can be incredibly effective and can help anglers catch a variety of fish species

- **Use live bait:** Using live bait can be an effective way to entice fish and increase your chances of catching a variety of fish species. Depending on the fish you're targeting, you can use live bait such as worms, minnows, or crickets. Live bait can be used with a variety of fishing techniques, including fly fishing and traditional spin fishing.

Fun Fact

Did you know that SUP was originally practiced in Hawaii as a means of transportation and for surfing?

Today, SUP has become a popular recreational activity worldwide, and many people enjoy it for its physical and mental health benefits as well as the fun and relaxation it provides. So, when you go on your first-ever SUP session, you're taking part in a fun and historical activity that has been enjoyed for centuries.

Chapter 2: Equipment

At the dawn of the COVID-19 pandemic—around the first quarter of 2021–SUP became one of people's favorite past times. While that's supposed to be a good thing, as it discourages people from living a sedentary lifestyle, it comes with a risky nature: The improper use of SUP equipment.

That said, one study–of many– insists that the importance of using proper equipment can't be stressed enough (Roberts, 2021). Without the right equipment, SUP is no longer a fun and worthwhile activity, but a dangerous and life-threatening hobby.

In this chapter, I'll walk you through the necessary equipment. If you're a beginner, I'll guide and prevent you from getting ahead of yourself. If you're a seasoned paddler, take notes and use the discussions to refresh your memory.

SUP Boards

Ready to hit the water?

If it's your first time stand-up paddleboarding, the excitement to go ahead and dive in with nothing but a random SUP board is understandable. Then again, it's not the best course of action.

If you insist otherwise, you may jeopardize your safety and not experience a quality SUP session.

So before anything else, pick out the *perfect* board for you. To do this, there's a lot to consider.

Depending on what kind of SUP activity you have in mind, you'll need to choose the right board.

You have four basic options.

- Option 1:

    If you're just starting out or plan on chillaxing with some fishing, then a **big, stable board** or **inflatable board** is the way to go. A larger board will typically be more stable in the water, making it easier for you to balance and avoid falling off. This can be especially helpful if you're new to SUP or if you're paddling in choppy or unpredictable waters. If you obtain an inflatable board, you can pack it nicely in the bag pack that comes with the board.

- Option 2:

    If you want something that can handle multiple SUP activities, like touring, racing, and yoga, then an **all-around board** is your jam. All around boards are designed to be versatile and adaptable, allowing you to use them for a variety of different SUP activities. One of their main advantages is that they can typically handle a wider range of water conditions than a board designed for a specific activity.

- Option 3:

    If you want more excitement like racing or downwinding, a long, narrow, and thick **race** or **downwind board** is the best for you. It comes in 12 or 14 foot in length and is designed for the purpose.

- Option 4:

    Ready to shred some serious waves like a pro? Then you'll need a **performance board** which is typically shorter and narrower than all around boards, with a pointed nose and a rocker—a curvature from nose to tail—designed to allow the board to ride over the waves smoothly and easily. The rails—edges of the board—are also designed to provide maximum maneuverability and control, allowing you to make quick turns and cutbacks as you ride the waves.

Once you start looking for a board, you may find a wider range of options than just the four options. You will find more information on SUP boards and related topics below.

Fun Fact

In Hawaii some advanced paddlers use regular long surfboards for SUP. In case you are not familiar with surfing, standing on a surfboard on flatwater is not easy. Can you imagine how difficult it is to stand on the board all the time?

Inflatable or regular SUP board?

Inflatable SUP boards and regular SUP hard boards have their own unique advantages and disadvantages. The choice between the two will largely depend on your personal preferences and intended use.

Inflatable SUP board:

Pros:

- Easy to transport and pack in a compact size
- Lightweight and can be carried in a backpack
- Durable and resistant to damage from impacts or rough handling during travel
- Can be used in various water conditions, including whitewater and flatwater
- Often less expensive than hard boards

Cons:

- Takes longer to set up and inflate than a hard board
- May not provide the same level of stability and rigidity as a hard board
- Can be affected by temperature changes, which may affect the air pressure and performance
- May require more maintenance, such as cleaning and drying properly after use and before storage

Regular SUP hard board:

Pros:

- Provides a more stable and rigid platform for paddling
- Offers better performance and speed in most water conditions
- Generally easier and faster to set up and use compared to inflatable boards
- Often preferred for surfing and racing

Cons:

- Heavy and bulky, making them more difficult to transport and store
- Prone to damage from impacts or rough handling during travel
- May require special storage or transportation arrangements, such as a roof rack or trailer
- More expensive than inflatable boards

Material and Repair

The riding experience of SUP can vary depending on the type of material used in the construction of the SUP board and the shape and size of the board.

Different materials are used to make the layers of SUP boards, and each material has its advantages and disadvantages. The type of material used depends on the intended use and the weight and personal preference of the paddler.

Here are some of the most common materials used to make SUP boards:

- **Core material and coating:** PU or PE (polyurethane blanks with polyester resin or epoxy resin) is commonly used and is cheaper than hollow wood or EPS foam, which is lighter, eco-friendly, and better suited for high performance.

    Polyester resin is cheaper than EPS resin but only makes the board look good when it's new as it ages quickly, while EPS resin is more durable and lasts longer. PVC material is used for inflatable boards, which are popular among beginners or some paddlers for specific usage.

    Inflatable SUP boards can be inflated and deflated for easy transport and storage. They are lightweight and durable and can withstand impact from rocks and other obstacles.

    As a result, they're ideal for travel and for paddlers who want to explore different bodies of water. However, take note that inflatable SUP boards are not as rigid as solid boards and may not perform as well in certain conditions.

- **Inner and outer layers:** Soft top, thermoplastic, fiberglass, carbon fiber, wooden stringer, and wood or bamboo veneer are used for wrapping the core portion to make the board.

  The combination of materials defines the intended usage and changes the weight, strength, and value of the board.

  Carbon fiber is considered the most durable and expensive material and can be used partially on the board to reduce the cost.

- **Repair:** small damage can be fixed easily with the right resin available at a DIY store or a ding repair kit available at a surf shop depending on the material of the board. For example, epoxy resin can be used on polyester or fiberglass boards. On the other hand, polyester or fiberglass resin cannot be used on the epoxy because it destroys the foam.

  If you are comfortable fixing your board, it will be the cheapest and fastest way. If not, you can take your board to a repair place or surf shop for repair. The repair time depends on the severity of the damage, the material of the board, and the availability of the shop.

  For your first board of any intended usage, look around and ask experts which board is most suitable for you. Just remember that there is not a single board that works for all conditions perfectly. There are a wide variety of SUP boards in the market available for different intended usages.

Fins: Fin Placement and Fin Box

According to Caranto (2022), one of the things that has the biggest impact on your experience and performance is your board's fin setup.

While beginners may not initially think too much about the fin setup of their board, as they progress and gain more experience, it becomes an important factor to consider when purchasing a new board.

Thankfully, many boards offer different fin setups. The goal is to suit the needs and preferences of different riders.

If you're just starting out, you may not need to worry too much about the fins on your board, but as you progress, the fin setup can make a big difference in your ability to maneuver and control your board on the water.

The placement of the fin can greatly impact the way the board handles, and depending on the type of paddling you plan to do, it can be placed in three different positions: forward, middle, or back.

- **Forward:** Once you've inserted the fin into the board, you can slide it forward towards the nose of the board. Placing the fin forward will increase the board's maneuverability, allowing for easier turns in either direction.

  However, if you plan on paddling in a straight line or going on a longer ride, placing the fin in the middle or back position may be more suitable for improved tracking and stability. Choosing the right fin position can greatly enhance your SUP experience, so consider the type of paddling you'll be doing before making a decision.

- **Middle:** For a casual SUP ride, it's recommended to keep your fin centered in the fin box. This position offers improved tracking and stability, making it easier to maintain a straight path and stay balanced on the board.

  However, if you plan on engaging in more dynamic activities like surfing or maneuvering through choppy waters, adjusting the fin position may be necessary to optimize performance. By carefully considering the conditions and activities you'll be encountering, you can find the right fin placement to enhance your SUP experience.

- **Back:** To decrease the maneuverability of your board, position the fin towards the back of the fin box and towards the tail of the board. This configuration will increase the board's stiffness, allowing it to maintain a straight path for longer periods of time.

    However, note that this position may be less suitable for activities that require frequent turning. By experimenting with different fin positions and considering your preferred paddling style, you can find the right balance between stability and maneuverability to optimize your SUP experience.

There are also many different types of fins and setups to choose from, and some boards even offer multiple fin boxes to allow for different configurations.

For example, some boards may have five fin boxes, providing a range of setup options to suit different riding styles and conditions.

It's of utmost importance you choose the right type of fin box for your board when purchasing new fins.

There are two main types of fin boxes:

1. **FCS (Fin Control System) box:** FCS is a type of fin box used in surfboard and SUP construction. The idea is to enable easy installation and removal of fins.

    It is a widely-used standard. It comes with two tabs that are inserted into the box and locked in place with screws. There are different FCS fin types. Check which type is used for your board before purchase.

2. **Futures box:** This system is a popular choice among those who wish to change their board fins

without requiring extra tools. It comes with a simple installation process that involves a single tab and screws for secure attachment.

If you're paddleboarding solely for fun, you might disregard the importance of picking the right fin box. However, to be safe, you'll need to make sure you choose your board that has the type of fin box you need.

Rail Guard

A rail guard is a useful accessory for protecting the rails or edges of your SUP board from damage caused by rocks, paddle strikes, and other hazards.

Here are some tips to help you choose the right rail guard for your SUP board:

- **Consider the material:** Rail guards can be made from a variety of materials, including rubber, PVC, and foam.

    Rubber rail guards are typically the most durable and can withstand heavy use, while foam rail guards are lightweight and provide a soft cushion for your board. Meanwhile, PVC rail guards offer a good balance of durability and cushioning.

- **Read reviews:** Before purchasing a rail guard, read reviews from other paddlers to see how the product performs and whether it is worth the investment.

Surface

Having a reliable and non-slip surface on your board is of utmost importance. It can help you stay safe and maintain control while riding the waves.

In traditional surfing, surfboards are commonly waxed to provide grip for the rider's feet, which helps maintain balance and control while catching waves.

However, SUP has a different approach.

Instead of wax, most SUP boards feature tracking pads that offer a non-slip surface, allowing paddlers to maintain balance and control without the need for additional wax.

If you prefer, you can still apply wax to the nose of the board to add extra grip when walking to the nose.

It's up to you to choose the right wax for your board and water temperature, as the wrong wax can make the board slippery, causing instability.

Alternatively, some SUP boards have a special finish that eliminates the need for wax or pads, providing a reliable and non-slip surface straight out of the box.

Whether you're using wax, pads, or a specialized finish, it's crucial to ensure that your SUP board has a non-slip surface. It helps you stay safe and in control while riding the waves or cruising around on the water.

Paddle

Pick a paddle that is the appropriate length for your height, the type of paddling you'll be doing, and most importantly your personal preference. It is easier said than done. Finding the right paddle for you can be challenging, just as much as finding the right board can be.

Here are some tips to help you:

- **Opt for durable materials:** Look for paddles made of durable materials, such as carbon fiber or fiberglass, which can withstand wear and tear over time.

- **Check the weight:** Choose a paddle that is lightweight enough to prevent fatigue during long paddles but still sturdy enough to provide sufficient power. However, lightweight paddles are more expensive than heavyweight paddles.

- **Shaft length:** Choose the right length for your intended usage. It is always relative to your height, thickness of your board, and other factors that change the experience of paddling. There is not a perfect chart that works for everyone to find the right paddle. However, paddle manufacturers and experts suggest somewhere between 6 to 10 inches longer than the height of the paddler. It depends on the overall paddle design and construction, your skill level, physical strength, intended usage, and your preference. A rule of thumb: it is usually shorter for surfing and longer for touring or racing.

- **Shaft design:** There is some variety in shaft designs. First, there are fixed and adjustable single piece, two-piece and three-piece paddles. From the performance perspective, fixed single piece paddles work the best, but some adjustable two-piece, or three-piece paddles are still good in addition to their adjustability and portability. Using an adjustable paddle is the best if you want to change the length of your paddle depending on the intended usage like sharing the paddle with multiple paddlers, or using the paddle for both touring and surfing. A two-piece or three-piece paddle is the best for traveling. Second, there are different shaft shapes. For adjustable paddles, there are different types of locking devices used to connect and disconnect pieces. Lastly, the shaft shape is usually rounded for most paddles but can be oval.

- **Grip design:** The top end of the paddle is called the "grip". It looks the same across all paddles but it is not the case. The best way to find the right grip for you is to try different grips and find which one works the best for you.

- **Blade design:** The bottom of the paddle is called the "blade". Consider the blade design, as it can affect your paddling experience. Just like the length of paddle, you need to find the right blade that works best for you. It depends on your weight, strength, intended usage, and your preference. A rule of thumb is that it is usually bigger for surfing and smaller for touring or racing

Leash

A leash keeps you connected to your SUP board and prevents it from washing away or hitting others in the water if you fall off. They also enhance safety by keeping you close to your board and help you recover quickly after a wipeout.

As it serves a key purpose in keeping you safe and connected to your SUP board, it's important to choose it wisely.

What can you do?

- **Go with the right length:** Select a leash that has the same length as the length of your board. It should allow you to move around freely and safely. If it is longer than the length of your board, it is more dangerous for others around you to get hit by your board. If it is shorter than the length of your board, it is more dangerous for you to get hit by your board.

- **Choose a comfortable ankle cuff:** The ankle cuff should fit snugly but should not be too tight, and it should be made of comfortable materials to avoid chafing. Remember the cuff will become loose when it's wet.

- **Check the leash cord:** Be sure the leash cord is made of durable and strong materials that can withstand strong impact or tension.

- **Straight or coil type? There are two leash types:** one is a straight leash which is the standard type and the other is a coil leash which keeps it out of the water when it is not stretched to avoid dragging. You can use either type if you are just touring on flatwater. Coil leashes are designed for flatwater or racing. Use the straight type for any other intended usage for your safety.

Carrier

A carrier is used to transport your SUP board from one location to another, protecting it from damage during transportation. It can be a backpack, wheeled bag, or roof rack system, depending on your preference and the distance you need to travel.

Tips to help you:

- **Be mindful of the weight and size:** Choose a carrier that can accommodate your board's weight and size and that you can handle easily.

- **Pick padded straps:** Look for a carrier with padded straps to provide comfort while carrying your board over long distances.

- **Aim for a sturdy design:** The carrier should be sturdy and durable, with a design that ensures that your board stays securely in place during transport.

Fun Fact

Did you know that demo boards are usually the most popular boards at paddleboard events because people love trying out different boards before making a purchase?

It's a great way to test out the feel and features of different boards and find the perfect fit for your paddling needs.

Chapter 3: Gear, Safety Measures and Basic Skills

According to *12 Safety Tips for Safe Stand-up Paddle Boarding* (2022), safety should always be a top priority when it comes to SUP. Having the right equipment helps guarantee that.

From the right paddle to the proper footwear and life jacket, each piece of equipment plays a vital role in your SUP adventure.

If you skimp on quality when it comes to your gear, you'll end up with subpar equipment that can increase the risk of injury or other accidents.

So, take the time to invest in equipment. With reliable and high-quality equipment, you can make the most of your time on the water.

In this chapter, I'll help you. We'll discuss all the essential SUP gear and more. We'll talk about what they are, what they do, and everything else that you need to know.

This way, you'll have everything you need to know before you go on the water.

Gear

Be prepared with the right gear when stand-up paddleboarding, especially since you may end up in the water for an extended period of time. The gear you choose should be based on the location where you're paddling.

For example, if you're in an area with four seasons, you may need to switch up your gear depending on the temperature.

In colder waters like the West Coast, a thicker wetsuit (4-5mm), gloves, and booties may be necessary year-round. In warmer waters like Hawaii, swimwear with a rash guard or surf vest may suffice.

Comfort is key, so be sure to choose gear that allows for ample shoulder movement.

Here are factors worth considering:

- **Style:** SUP has become increasingly popular, and as such, there are more options than ever when it comes to style. Consider what looks good to you and what fits your personal aesthetic.

- **Accessibility:** If you have any physical limitations, look for gear that is designed to accommodate your needs. For example, some companies make adaptive paddling equipment for people with disabilities.

- **Multi-functionality:** Invest in gear that can serve many purposes. An example is a paddle that you can use for easy storage and transport or a board that you can use for paddling and yoga. It can help you increase your versatility on the water.

Life Jacket or Vest

A life jacket or vest is an essential piece of equipment for any SUP enthusiast. Not only is it a legal requirement in many areas, but it can also be a lifesaver in the event of an accident.

Here's a step-by-step guide to help you choose the right life jacket or vest for your SUP adventures:

- **Determine the activity level:** Choose a life jacket or vest that's rated for your activity level. For SUP, a Type III Personal Flotation Device (PFD) is recommended. This type of PFD is designed for water sports and provides a good balance of comfort and safety. If you prefer something comfy, you can use a Type III inflatable PFD which is designed to inflate when submerged in water. However, you need to replace the cartridge after inflation every time.

- **Check the fit:** A life jacket or vest should fit snugly but not be too tight. It should also be adjustable to fit different body sizes and shapes. Try on different sizes and styles to find the one that fits you best.
- **Consider the features:** Different life jackets or vests come with different features. Think about what you need. For example, some may have pockets for storing small items, while others may have a whistle or other signaling device attached.
- **Wear it at all times:** It's important to wear your life jacket or vest at all times while on the water except when you are surfing. Accidents can happen even to experienced paddlers. By choosing a quality and properly fitted life jacket or vest, you can enjoy a safe and comfortable SUP experience.

Impact Vest

An impact vest is designed to absorb the shock of impact and protect your rib cage and vital organs from injury. Choose a vest that fits snugly and provides optimal coverage and protection. Thicker vests provide more warmth and protection in colder waters.

Helmet

A helmet is designed to protect the head from impact during falls or collisions. It acts as a shock absorber and can prevent serious head injuries such as concussions or skull fractures.

Helmets can also protect the face and eyes from injury in the event of a fall.

Here's a step-by-step guide to help you choose the right helmet SUP adventures:

- **Determine the type of water conditions:** Consider the water conditions you'll be paddling in. If you'll be in rough waters or surf, you'll need a helmet that provides extra protection for your head.

- **Look for water-specific helmets:** Choose a helmet specifically designed for water sports, as they are typically made from lightweight and impact-resistant materials that can withstand the harsh elements of the water. Make sure the helmet is approved by the appropriate safety standard agency.

- **Check the fit:** A helmet should fit snugly but not be too tight. It should also have adjustable straps to fit different head sizes and shapes. Try on different sizes and styles to find the one that fits you best.

- **Consider the style and design:** Helmets come in various colors and designs, allowing you to express your personal style while staying safe on the water.

Wear them at all times: It's crucial to wear your helmet and impact vest at all times especially when you are learning how to paddle on a foil board or when you are paddling in rough conditions. Accidents can happen to anyone, and having the proper safety gear can prevent serious injuries and save your life.

Other Useful Items

When heading out for a SUP adventure, it's important to have useful items on hand for convenience. These items can save you time, make your experience more enjoyable, and even help you stay safe in case of an emergency.

Waterproof Watch

A waterproof watch can be a useful piece of gear for SUP, as it can help you keep track of time, monitor your heart rate, and even provide GPS tracking.

When choosing a waterproof watch for SUP, there are several factors to consider:

- **Water resistance rating:** The watch should have a water resistance rating of at least 50 meters, which means it can withstand being submerged in water up to that depth.

- **Durability:** A watch for SUP should be durable enough to withstand rough conditions and potential impacts from water hazards.

- **Visibility:** The watch should have a high-contrast display that is easy to read in different lighting conditions, including direct sunlight and low light.

- **Features:** Consider what features are important to you, such as GPS tracking, heart rate monitoring, and timers.

- **Comfort:** The watch should fit comfortably on your wrist and not interfere with your movement while paddling.

- **Battery life:** Check the battery life of the watch to ensure it can last for the duration of your paddling sessions.

- **Compatibility:** If you plan to sync the watch with a smartphone, make sure it is compatible with your device and any apps you plan to use.
- **Brand reputation:** Consider the reputation of the watch brand and read reviews to ensure you are purchasing a quality product that meets your needs.

Waterproof Sunglasses

For those seeking an elegant means of shielding their eyes from the sun's glare and water splashes, waterproof sunglasses offer a compelling solution. These sunglasses present similar benefits to standard sunglasses, including polarized lenses and UV protection, with the added advantage of being able to withstand a fall off your board or sudden wave impact.

Notably, they can be worn on the beach or while relaxing after a long SUP session.

Why settle for ordinary sunglasses when you can enjoy a pair capable of overcoming any obstacle? Waterproof sunglasses provide superior eye protection while also enhancing your style.

It is therefore recommended that you add a pair of waterproof sunglasses to your SUP kit for a fashionable and practical accessory to your water activities.

Here is a step-by-step guide on how to choose waterproof sunglasses:

- **Look for UV protection:** The first thing to consider when choosing waterproof sunglasses is the level of UV protection they offer. Look for shades with a high level of UV protection, as this will help to protect your eyes from harmful sun rays.
- **Check the lens quality:** Another important factor to consider is the quality of the lens. Polarized lenses

are a great option as they reduce glare and provide better vision on the water.

Additionally, some waterproof sunglasses have lenses that are scratch-resistant or shatterproof, which can be particularly helpful if you're accident-prone. Make sure you attach a strap and floatable object to your sunglasses in case you fall off the board.

- **Choose a comfortable fit:** Look for waterproof sunglasses with a comfortable fit that won't slide down your face or cause discomfort during long paddles. Consider the shape and size of the frames, as well as the fit around your ears and nose.

- **Consider the style:** Waterproof sunglasses come in a variety of styles and colors, so choose a pair that reflects your personal taste and matches your SUP gear. Some popular styles include aviators, wayfarers, and sport sunglasses.

- **Look for durability:** Waterproof sunglasses are designed to withstand the elements, so look for shades made from high-quality, durable materials that can handle the wear and tear of water sports. Some waterproof sunglasses are also designed with added features, such as non-slip grips or floating frames, to make them even more durable and practical for SUP.

Portable Shower

When you have a long SUP session, especially if you fall off the board many times, you probably want to take a shower before heading back home.

If there are no public showers around, a portable shower can come in handy after a SUP session.

Here are some factors to consider when choosing a portable shower:

- **Water capacity:** Check the water capacity of the shower to ensure it's enough for your needs.
- **Ease of use:** Consider how easy it is to use and set up, and whether it requires electricity or batteries.
- **Water temperature:** Look for a shower that can heat water if you prefer warm showers.
- **Durability:** Consider the quality of the materials and the ability of the shower to withstand outdoor conditions.
- **Portability:** Consider the size and weight of the shower, and whether it's easy to pack and transport on your SUP adventures.

Waterproof Bag

A waterproof bag is an essential accessory for anyone who wants to keep their belongings dry while enjoying outdoor activities. Whether you're going to the beach, hiking, or kayaking, a waterproof bag can protect your phone, keys, wallet, and other valuables from getting wet.

It can also keep your wet gear and towels after your SUP session.

Moreover, a waterproof bag can be handy in case of an emergency, such as if you need to store food or supplies for a longer trip or if you need to keep important documents or medication dry.

Waterproof bags are available in various types and sizes, making it easy to find one that suits your needs.

Here are the different types of waterproof bags:

- **Waterproof pouches:** These are small, compact bags that can hold your phone, keys, or other small items. They are usually made of PVC or nylon and can be carried around your neck or waist.

- **Dry bags:** These are larger bags that can hold your clothes, towels, and other gear. They are made of durable materials such as vinyl or polyester and come in different sizes and shapes, including backpacks, duffel bags, and roll-top bags.

- **Waterproof backpacks:** These are backpacks specifically designed to keep your gear dry. They are made of waterproof materials and feature welded seams to prevent water from seeping in. Some waterproof backpacks also come with padded straps and back panels for added comfort.

- **Waterproof cases:** These are protective cases that can hold your phone, tablet, or other electronic devices. They are usually made of hard plastic or silicone and come with a secure locking mechanism to prevent water from getting inside.

Leggings

Leggings are a popular and versatile option for SUP, offering both coverage and flexibility. During the season of jellyfish, those are super useful to protect yourself from being stung by a jellyfish.

When selecting leggings for your next SUP session, there are several factors to consider:

- **Material:** Opt for leggings made from quick-drying, moisture-wicking fabrics to keep you comfortable and dry on the water. Look for materials that offer UPF protection to protect your skin from the sun's harmful rays.

- **Fit:** Choose leggings with a secure, supportive waistband that won't slip or sag while you're paddling. High-waisted or adjustable waistbands can provide extra support and coverage.

- **Length:** Consider the weather conditions and your personal preference when choosing the length of your leggings. Full-length leggings offer maximum coverage, while cropped leggings provide more breathability in warmer temperatures.
- **Thermal properties:** In colder temperatures, select leggings with thermal properties or layer up with waterproof pants over your leggings for added warmth and protection.
- **Style:** Leggings come in a wide variety of colors and designs, so choose a pair that reflects your personality and matches your other SUP gear.

Hooded Changing Towel or Poncho

A hooded changing towel or poncho can be a great item for any SUP enthusiast. These versatile pieces of gear allow you to change out of your wet clothes and into something dry and warm while still maintaining your modesty in public places.

Hooded changing towels and ponchos come in a variety of sizes and styles to suit different preferences. Some are made from soft and absorbent materials like terry cloth or microfiber, while others are designed to be quick-drying and lightweight for maximum portability.

One of the biggest perks of a hooded changing towel or a poncho is that you can wear them like a robe. They help make it effortless to get out of your clothes, wet without exposure to the elements or other people.

The hood helps to dry your hair and keep you warm, and often, the changing towel and often the changing towel or poncho will have a large front pocket for storing your phone, keys, or other small items.

Electric Pump

An electric pump is a delight for anyone who regularly inflates their SUP board. Not only does it save time and effort, but it also ensures that your board is inflated to the correct pressure for optimal performance and stability on the water.

Here's a step-by-step guide on how to use your pump:

- **Choose the right electric pump:** There are two main types of electric pumps: battery-powered and plug-in models. Consider the portability and convenience of each option, as well as any additional features like automatic shut-off or LED displays.

- **Prepare your inflatable board:** Lay your board flat on a stable surface and ensure the valve is free of debris or sand. This will help prevent damage to the valve and ensure a proper seal for inflation.

- **Attach the pump to the valve:** Connect the hose of the electric pump to the valve on your board. Ensure a secure fit to prevent air leaks during inflation.

- **Set the desired pressure:** Determine the ideal PSI for your board and adjust the settings on the electric pump accordingly. Most electric pumps have settings that allow you to select the desired pressure and will automatically stop inflating once that pressure is reached.

- **Turn on the pump:** Power on the electric pump and let it inflate your board to the desired pressure. Monitor the progress and adjust the pressure as necessary to achieve optimal performance and stability on the water.

- **Disconnect and store the pump:** Once the SUP board is fully inflated, disconnect the pump from the valve and store it properly. Follow manufacturer instructions for care and maintenance to ensure long-lasting performance from your electric pump.

Surf Wax

Surf wax can be an accessory for SUP surfing, providing traction and preventing slipping on the board.

Here are the steps to select and apply surf wax:

- **Consider the water temperature and type of board:** Different surf waxes are designed for different water temperatures and board types. Softer waxes work best for warm water, while harder waxes are better for colder water. Additionally, some waxes are formulated for use on specific types of boards, such as epoxy or soft-top boards.

- **Use base wax first for brand new boards:** There are waxes for base coating and daily use for different water temperatures.

- **Clean the board surface:** Before applying surf wax, clean the surface of the board with a damp cloth to remove any dirt, sand, or debris. This will ensure that the wax adheres properly to the board.

- **Apply the surf wax:** Begin by holding the wax against the board's surface and rubbing it in small circular motions. Apply it evenly around the nose if the board already has tracking pads. The wax will start to form small bumps or ridges on the board's surface. Apply enough wax to create a thin layer, but not so much that it feels thick or clumpy. Avoid over-waxing because it can make the board too slippery. When you are using base wax, apply regular wax over the base wax.

- **Add more wax as needed:** The amount of wax you'll need depends on the size of the board and the conditions you'll be surfing in. For colder water or larger boards, you may need to apply more wax to ensure adequate traction.

- **Clean the board's surface regularly:** Dirt and grime buildup can affect the grip of your board, so it's crucial to clean it regularly. You can use a mild detergent and warm water to clean the board's surface. Avoid using harsh chemicals that can damage the board's surface.

Super Basic Skills

Having super basic skills is vital for anyone who wants to have a worthwhile time stand-up paddleboarding.

Below are the basic skills worth mastering:

- **Proper paddling technique:** Knowing how to hold the paddle, where to place your hands, and how to use the power of your core muscles is essential to paddling efficiently and smoothly.

- **How to climb back onto the board:** To ensure that you can safely get back on the board after falling off, it's important to know different techniques like the knee climb or board flip to avoid causing damage to the board or injury to yourself.

- **How to stand:** To successfully stand up on the board from a kneeling or seated position, it's important to know how to place your hands on the board to push up while maintaining balance and stability.

- **Balance on the board:** To maintain balance and stability on the board, it's important to keep your feet shoulder-width apart, bend your knees slightly, and distribute your weight evenly on the board.

- **Turning:** Knowing how to turn the board by using different strokes, such as the forward sweep, back sweep, and cross-bow turn, is essential to navigating through different water conditions.

- **Safe falling:** Knowing how to fall safely involves jumping clear of the board, keeping your arms and legs close to your body, and surfacing safely to prevent injury.

- **Awareness of water conditions:** To ensure your safety and plan your paddling route accordingly, it's important to know how to read the water conditions, including wind, waves, currents, and tides.

There are many teaching videos on paddling and riding techniques available online and SUP lessons for different skill levels available at many places. It is best you learn basic skills first and move on to the next level of your journey.

Fun Fact

According to research, the world's longest SUP ride occurred in 2017. That time, adventurer Bart de Zwart paddled from Ketchikan, Alaska, to Bellingham, Washington, completing the journey in just over three weeks.

Along the way, he battled strong winds, rough seas, and even encountered some friendly dolphins. It just goes to show that with the right equipment and plenty of determination, stand-up paddleboarding can take you on some pretty epic adventures! (Paddle Board World Records to Beat | Aquaplanet Sport, n.d.)

Chapter 4: Speed - Downwind, Race, and Rapids (Whitewater)

Whitewater SUP combines the thrill of whitewater rafting with the challenge and excitement of SUP. This activity requires a combination of balance, strength, and quick reflexes as you navigate rapids and waves while standing on your board.

Talk about an exhilarating way to experience the beauty of nature and test your skills against the power of the water.

In this chapter, we'll focus on speed as we discuss downwind, race, and rapids. We'll cover what they are, what makes them special, and more. We'll also talk about a relevant fun fact to wrap things up.

Downwind

Downwind paddling involves using the wind to propel you forward on the water, creating a fast and exhilarating ride. This type of paddling is particularly popular in coastal areas.

It requires skill and experience, as you need to be able to read the wind and waves, anticipate changes in conditions, and adjust your paddle strokes and body positioning accordingly.

Once you've mastered the technique, downwind paddling can be an incredibly fun and satisfying way to enjoy the beauty and power of the ocean or lake.

Below are some tips to help you get started.

- **Paddle stroke:** To maximize your speed and maintain momentum, use a high-angle paddle stroke and engage your core muscles. This will help you generate more power with each stroke, especially in choppy conditions.

- **Reach forward:** Reach your paddle as far forward as possible before each stroke to catch the wind and use it to your advantage.
- **Catch the bumps:** Look for wind-generated swells and try to catch the bump when it is passing underneath you. Once you're on the bump, you can pick up speed and try to catch another moving fast before losing the speed.
- **Quick recovery:** Keep your paddle close to the board to recover quickly after each stroke. This will help you maintain your balance and speed and be ready to catch the next bump.
- **Alternate sides:** Alternate your paddle strokes on both sides of the board to maintain your balance and reduce fatigue. This will help you keep your speed and momentum going, even during long downwind runs.

Typically, downwind boards come in sizes of 12 or 14 feet in length. There are All Round models that work for both racing and down-winding as well. If you can use a rental board or borrow someone's board, it is best to try it first before purchasing one. You may experience the difference between different models with the same length.

How to Downwind

While downwind paddling and surfing share some similarities, there are key differences in their techniques. In downwind paddling, the goal is to catch and ride wind-generated swells, rather than ocean waves. This requires a different approach to positioning, paddling, and maneuvering on the board.

Additionally, downwind paddling often involves longer, sustained rides, which require a different level of endurance and stamina compared to the quick bursts of energy in surfing. Successful downwind paddlers also need to be able to read the water and wind conditions to effectively navigate the course.

How to Ride Bumps on the River

Riding bumps on a river can be a thrilling experience, but it requires skill and technique to do it safely and effectively.

Here are some tips:

- **Be alert:** Constantly scan the water ahead and anticipate where the bumps will form. Keep your eyes on the horizon and watch for changes in the water's surface.

- **Stay loose:** As you approach a bump, relax your body and bend your knees to absorb the impact. Let your board move up and down with the water, and avoid resisting it.

- **Use your paddle:** Use your paddle to brace and maintain your balance as you ride over the bumps. Keep your paddle close to your body and use it to stabilize yourself when necessary.

- **Hone your skills:** Riding bumps on a river takes practice. Start with smaller bumps and gradually work up to bigger ones as you gain confidence and skill.

How to Ride Bumps on the Ocean

Cruising through bumps on the ocean can be an exhilarating experience, but it requires a combination of skill, timing, and strategy.

Here are some tips:

- **Read the water:** Observe the water ahead of you and look for areas where the bumps are forming. Pay

attention to the direction and strength of the wind and the angle of the swell.
- **Position yourself:** Position yourself in front of the bump and paddle hard to catch it. Keep your weight forward on the board to maintain your momentum.
- **Watch your balance:** As you ride the bump, stay centered on the board and keep your weight balanced. Use your paddle to brace and maintain your stability.
- **Look ahead:** Keep your eyes on the horizon and anticipate where the next bump will form. Use this information to position yourself for the next ride.
- **Practice:** Riding bumps on the ocean takes practice. Start with smaller bumps and gradually work up to bigger ones as you gain confidence and skill. Remember to always prioritize safety and follow the rules of the water.

Top Five Unforgettable Downwind Races in History

Downwind races are some of the most exciting and challenging events in the sport of SUP. These races typically involve paddling with the wind and waves at your back, which can generate incredible speed and create adrenaline-pumping moments.

Here are five of the top downwind races in the world:

1. **Maui 2 Molokai:** This iconic race takes place in Hawaii, where competitors paddle 32 miles from the island of Maui to the island of Molokai. The race is known for its strong winds, big waves, and beautiful scenery, attracting some of the top SUP athletes in the world.
2. **Gorge Paddle Challenge:** Held in Hood River, Oregon, this race is known for its challenging

downwind conditions and stunning views of the Columbia River Gorge. Competitors paddle a 6-mile course through the gorge, which is known for its strong winds and choppy waters.

3. **The Carolina Cup:** This annual event takes place in Wrightsville Beach, North Carolina, and features a variety of SUP races, including a challenging 13.2-mile downwind race. The course takes paddlers through the Cape Fear River and out to the open ocean, where they can catch some incredible waves and wind.

4. **The Doctor:** This race takes place in Western Australia and covers a distance of around 17.40 miles from Rottnest Island to Sorrento Beach. The course features some challenging conditions, including strong winds, big waves, and tricky currents, making it a true test of skill and endurance.

5. **Molokai 2 Oahu:** Similar to the Maui 2 Molokai race, this event takes paddlers on a 32-mile journey from Molokai to Oahu. The race is known for its tough conditions, including strong winds and challenging currents, and attracts some of the top SUP athletes from around the world.

Race

From an outsider's perspective, races are all about fun. A closer look tells you differently, though.

SUP races are the ultimate test of skill and endurance. It's a chance to challenge yourself, push your limits, and compete against others to see who's the fastest and most efficient paddler.

From short, adrenaline-fueled sprints to long-distance endurance races, there's a SUP race out there for everyone. You'll battle against the elements, navigate through choppy waters, and race alongside fellow paddlers in a high-stakes, high-energy event that will leave you feeling exhilarated and accomplished.

Here are tips to help you:

- **Focus:** It's important to stay focused on the race and not get distracted by other racers or your surroundings. Keep your attention on the race and your goals.
- **Paddle efficiently:** Work on paddling with efficiency to conserve your energy and stay ahead of the competition. Find a rhythm that works for you and focus on maintaining it throughout the race.
- **Choose the best line:** Be strategic in your course selection and choose the best line to minimize the distance you have to paddle. This will help you save time and energy.
- **Hydrate:** It's essential to stay hydrated during a race, even if the conditions are cool. Make sure you have a hydration plan in place before the race starts, and stick to it.
- **Stay positive:** Keeping a positive attitude can help you stay motivated and focused during the race. Focus on your strengths and stay confident in your abilities. Even if you fall behind, remember to keep pushing yourself and stay in the game.

Racing

If you're looking to increase your speed on the water, consider using a race board and tapping into your physical strength.

Typically, race boards come in sizes of 12 or 14 feet in length similar to downwind boards. So if you're looking to move quickly on the water, consider training with a race board and using your physical abilities to your advantage.

What can you get from racing?

- **Adrenaline rush:** Racing on a race board can be an incredibly exhilarating experience, especially when you're paddling with the wind and waves at your back. The rush of adrenaline you get from catching big waves and cruising at high speeds can be truly unforgettable.

- **Test of skill and endurance:** Racing requires a combination of physical fitness, technical skill, and mental focus. It's not just about paddling fast but also about navigating currents, reading the water, and making strategic decisions along the way. Racing can be a true test of your abilities and endurance.

- **Connection to nature:** Many SUP races take place in beautiful natural settings, such as oceans, lakes, and rivers. Racing can be a great way to connect with nature and appreciate the beauty of the world around you. You may encounter marine life, stunning vistas, and unique ecosystems along the way.

- **Camaraderie and community:** Participating in a race can be a great way to meet new people and connect with like-minded individuals. Whether you're racing against others or simply enjoying the experience together, SUP events can create a sense of camaraderie and community that can be truly rewarding.

- **Sense of accomplishment:** Finishing a race can be an incredibly satisfying and rewarding experience, especially if you've pushed yourself to your limits along the way.

Whether you're racing against others or simply trying to beat your personal best, crossing the finish line can give you a sense of accomplishment and pride that will stay with you for a long time.

Participating in a SUP Race

Participating in a SUP race doesn't require professional skills. I've personally tried it and enjoyed the lively atmosphere of paddling alongside numerous others in open water.

The race can also challenge you to paddle further, pushing you to achieve more.

To me, it feels like a marathon for SUP, but with a fun and friendly vibe.

Below is a list of things to remember when participating in a SUP race:

- **Be prepared:** Make sure to bring all necessary equipment, such as a properly sized board, paddle, leash, and life jacket. Also, be sure to bring water, snacks, and any other essentials you may need during the race.

- **Warm-up:** Take some time to warm up before the race to prevent injury and get your muscles ready. This can include stretching, light jogging, and a few practice paddles.

- **Follow the rules:** Pay attention to the race rules, including course instructions and safety guidelines. This will help ensure a fair and safe race for all participants.

- **Pace yourself:** Find a comfortable pace and maintain it throughout the race. Don't push yourself too hard too early, as this can lead to exhaustion and burnout later on.

- **Have fun:** SUP races are a great opportunity to challenge yourself, meet new people, and have fun. So, relax, enjoy the scenery, and remember to have fun while paddling your way to the finish line!

Tips

Maintaining a low center of gravity, using a consistent and powerful paddle stroke, and staying balanced and stable on the board are all important things to remember when racing.

It's also crucial to pay attention to the wind and current conditions and to adjust your strategy accordingly. Practice and training are essential for mastering the intricacies of paddling on a race board, but with dedication and persistence, anyone can become a skilled and competitive paddler.

According to De Haan (2020), here are some tips to help you paddle on a race board like a champion:

- **Get comfortable:** Before you even start paddling, make sure you're comfortable on your race board. Adjust your foot position and ensure your stance is stable and balanced.

- **Use your whole body:** Paddling on a race board requires more than just arm strength. Use your entire body, including your legs and core, to generate power and maximize your speed.

- **Keep your strokes efficient:** Don't waste energy with inefficient strokes. Keep your strokes smooth and consistent, focusing on a clean entry and a strong pull through the water.

- **Maintain a high cadence:** In a race, speed is everything. To go fast on a race board, you need to maintain a high cadence or stroke rate. This means taking quick, efficient strokes to keep up your momentum.

- **Focus:** Paddling on a race board requires intense focus and concentration. Stay focused on your technique, your speed, and your strategy for the race. And don't forget to enjoy the experience: it's all about the journey, not just the finish line.

Paddle Through Rapids in the River

Paddling through rapids on a river can be insane. As you make your way through them, you'll feel the power of the water rushing beneath your board. You'll also experience the thrill of navigating through the fast-moving current.

Paddling through rapids for the first time can be a challenging even though you already know how to paddle in rough conditions. It's important to approach it with focus and caution and to keep your paddle strokes steady and consistent. Maintaining a low center of gravity and staying balanced on the board is crucial.

Be prepared to navigate through varying currents and obstacles, and don't hesitate to seek advice from experienced paddlers. With practice and persistence, conquering rapids can be an exhilarating and rewarding achievement.

Here are more tips to make the most out of paddling through rapids:

- **Scout the rapids:** Before embarking on your journey, make sure to scout the rapids and check for any potential hazards, such as rocks or debris. Look for eddies or calm spots to take a break or rest.
- **Start slow:** If you're new to paddling through rapids, start with easy rapids and gradually work your way up to more challenging ones. This will help

you build confidence and develop your skills without overwhelming yourself.

- **Use proper equipment:** Wear a helmet, PFD, and protective gear to ensure your safety during the paddle. Make sure your board is appropriate for the type of water you will be paddling on.

- **Be mindful of your body position:** Keep your weight centered over the board, and use your core muscles to maintain balance and stability. Lean back slightly to avoid catching the nose of the board and potentially capsizing.

- **Stock up on "paddle power":** Use powerful, sweeping strokes to move through the rapids, keeping your paddle low to the water to avoid catching on rocks. Use your feet to help steer and balance the board as you move through the current.

Inspiration

Paddling through rapids can provide both physical and mental benefits.

As a physical workout, it challenges your core and upper body strength. As a result, it can help improve your balance and coordination.

Mentally, it can boost your confidence and decision-making skills as you learn to navigate through fast-moving water and overcome obstacles. Additionally, the experience of being in nature and the rush of adrenaline can help reduce stress and promote a sense of relaxation and well-being.

What awaits you:

- **Heart-pounding journey:** Paddling through rapids on a SUP board can be a heart-pounding journey as you navigate through rough water, dodge obstacles, and ride the waves.

- **Physical challenge:** Paddling through rapids can be a challenging physical workout, as you use your core and upper body strength to navigate the water. It can be a great way to stay in shape and build your endurance.
- **New adventure:** Trying SUP in rapids can be exciting, even if you've been paddling for a while. It can help you break out of your routine, push your limits, and try something new and exhilarating.

Fun Fact

Did you know that you can ride the water in different ways for an adrenaline rush?

Downwind uses wind and bumps to propel a paddleboard. Racing is done in the open ocean with various watercraft. Whitewater paddling involves navigating rapids and turbulent water.

Chapter 5: Surfing

The excitement of an endless summer is alluring.

But when it comes to surfing, don't get ahead of yourself and take precautions. Before hitting the waves, make sure you know what you're doing and check the conditions of the surf spot.

Take a moment to observe the waves, the currents, and the other surfers. Don't rush into the water without assessing the situation, or you may find yourself in a dangerous predicament.

Remember, the key to a successful and safe surf session is preparation and awareness.

In this chapter, we'll dig through the subject of surfing. We'll talk about the basics of surfing, reasons to surf, how to be in a surf stance, and more.

Surfing 101

Did you know that the Hawaiian word for surfing, "he'e nalu," translates to "wave sliding"?

It's no surprise, then, that paddling is an essential part of surfing. That's according to an article about surf culture (*What Is Surf Culture in 2022?*, 2022).

In fact, before catching a wave, surfers spend most of their time paddling and positioning themselves to catch the perfect ride.

Reasons to Surf

People surf for various reasons, including the adrenaline rush, the connection to nature, the physical and mental benefits, and the social aspect of the sport. Surfing has also become a competitive sport, with various competitions held globally.

SUP boards for surfing come in different types and sizes, each suited for different types of waves and skill levels.

Long SUP boards, for example, are larger and easier to paddle, making them a great option for beginners.

Short SUP boards, on the other hand, are more maneuverable and suited for experienced surfers looking to perform tricks.

Pro Model SUP boards are also popular among advanced SUP surfers, as they offer more maneuverability like surfboards, but they are smaller and narrower than any other SUP boards which require a high level of skills.

Gear up!

As with SUP, wetsuits and other gear are also essential for surfing, as they keep surfers stay warm in the cold water and provide protection. Wetsuits come in different thicknesses and materials, depending on the water temperature and the surfer's preferences. Even in the warm weather like Hawaii, some SUP surfers use their vests or shorties to stay warm on a windy or cloudy day.

Choosing the right SUP surfboard and gear is necessary for a memorable SUP surfing experience. If you need help, seek advice from experienced surfers or professionals when selecting equipment.

Surf Stance

Your stance affects your balance, maneuverability, and control. It refers to how you position your feet on the board while holding a paddle, and it can significantly impact your performance on the water. Mastering the art of catching a wave in a surf stance requires practice and patience. Don't be discouraged if you don't succeed at first.

First you need to determine your dominant foot. You can do this by having someone gently push you from behind, and whichever foot you use to catch yourself instinctively is your dominant foot. If you're unsure, experiment with both stances to determine which one feels more comfortable for you.

Here's a step-by-step guide to getting your stance:

1. **Get ready:** Begin by standing in the center of the board with your feet shoulder-width apart and start paddling.

2. **Get in position:** You need to switch your position to the surf stance quickly by placing your dominant foot near the center and the other foot near the tail of the board while paddling on the side of your back foot.

3. **Angle your front foot:** Angle your front foot towards the nose of the board.

4. **Position your back foot:** Your back foot should be perpendicular to the board, with your toes pointing towards the side. This position allows you to generate the most power and control while riding waves.

5. **Maintain your balance:** Use paddle strokes to maintain your balance. Bending your knees helps you maintain your balance on the board and makes it easier to shift your weight quickly and turn the board when riding the wave.

Quick Turn

Turning your board quickly into the direction of the wave is essential for catching a wave. You need to get into the position to take off right before the wave starts breaking.

When you practicing the surf stance, add one more step to practice the quick turn. While standing in the surf stance, step back even further on your board so the nose of the board lifts from the water and the tail of the board goes underwater. The further back you step, the quicker you can turn. Paddle to turn the board while standing in a wide surf stance and bend your knees to maintain your balance.

Before trying to catch a wave, practice the surf stance and quick turn on flatwater.

Paddle Out

Paddling out can be challenging. However, if your heart is set on it, of course, you'll practice and get better at it. Remember to always stay focused, be mindful of your safety, and have a great time!

Here's a step-by-step guide on how to paddle out:

1. **Observe the waves:** Before you paddle out, take a moment to observe the waves. Look for patterns in the swell, identify where the waves are breaking, and locate the channel or the safest path to get out.

2. **Time your entry:** Timing is key when it comes to paddling out. Wait for a lull in the waves and start paddling toward the lineup. Avoid paddling out through the impact zone, where the waves are breaking.

3. **Use the rip current:** If there is a rip current, use it to your advantage. A rip current is a channel of water that flows away from the shore, and can help

you paddle out more easily. Paddle diagonally towards the rip, and it will take you out beyond the breaking waves.

4. **Keep your eyes open:** While you're paddling out, keep an eye on the waves. If a big set is coming toward you, paddle away to avoid getting caught in the impact zone.

5. **Be aware of others in the water:** When you're in the water, be aware of other surfers and paddlers around you. Look out for others who are riding a wave towards you and paddle away to avoid colliding with them. If you are a beginner, stay away from the lineup and practice on small waves inside.

6. **Stay calm:** Paddling out can be challenging, especially if the waves are big. If you are a beginner, stay away from big waves. If you get caught in the impact zone, stay calm, take a deep breath, and dive under the wave to avoid getting pummeled.

7. **Keep paddling:** Once you're past the impact zone, keep paddling until you reach flatwater. Find a spot where you're not in the way of other surfers, and wait for your turn to catch a wave. See surfing etiquette below.

Paddle into a Wave

To experience the thrill of SUP surfing, you need to learn how to select a wave to catch and how to position yourself before catching it. It'll make all the difference between a mediocre session and an epic one!

Here's a step-by-step guide on how to paddle into a wave on a SUP board:

1. **Look for a wave to catch:** Keep an eye out for incoming waves. Do not try to take the first wave but observe carefully how waves are breaking at the spot

and how others are surfing on the waves so that you know where to position yourself. If you are a beginner, look for a small wave inside of the spot but again observe how it breaks before trying to catch it. Usually you see similar breaking patterns of waves at one spot. Remember, wave conditions are different throughout the day and every day.

2. **Paddle into a wave:** When you know which wave you want to catch, paddle towards it but aim at slightly shoulder of the wave. Waves usually break from the peak to the shoulder on either side or both sides. Try to see where the wave breaks and where the peak is. The idea is you want to start catching the wave from slightly left or right of the peak. When you start from the peak and do not know how to turn quickly and properly, you may fall off right at the moment the wave breaks. If you are too far from the peak, you probably do not catch the wave. If the wave is very small, the peak is not even recognizable and it could be a wide area of the wave. In this case you can start from anywhere on the top of the wave.

3. **Get into position:** Turn your board around quickly into the direction of the wave. You need to keep paddling to maintain your balance and gain speed to match the speed of the wave. Ensure that you are far enough away from other surfers to avoid collisions.

4. **Start paddling:** To generate speed, keep paddling in the direction of the wave. Remember, to maintain your speed, paddle consistently. Avoid pausing your strokes, as this can slow down your board and cause you to lose momentum.

You need to know where to go and how to navigate yourself into the wave. So observing others who are catching waves always helps.

How to Catch a Wave

Catching a wave on a SUP surfboard is the ultimate thrill ride. But let's be real. Without the right paddling skills, you're not going to be catching much of anything!

Here's a step-by-step guide on how to do it:

1. **Start paddling:** Paddle toward the wave that you want to catch. Your aim is to catch up to the wave before it breaks.

2. **Get into position:** When you are close to the wave, turn your board quickly into the direction of the wave and start paddling.

3. **Surf stance:** When the wave begins to lift you up, switch to the surf stance and paddle using power strokes.

4. **Gain momentum:** Take a few quick and powerful strokes to gain momentum and lift yourself onto the wave.

5. **Ride the wave:** Keep your knees bent and your weight centered over the board. Use your paddle and body to maintain your balance and direction as you ride the wave. Enjoy the ride!

Once you're riding the wave, continue paddling to maintain your speed and momentum. Use your paddle to steer the board as needed, and adjust your weight distribution to stay balanced. If you are going too slow, move your back foot forward towards the middle of the board. If you are going too fast, move your back foot towards the tail to slow down.

If you want to turn, shift your weight to the side you want to turn toward, and use a sweeping stroke with your paddle to turn the board. Remember to keep your paddle close to the board to maintain stability.

Be aware of your surroundings and other surfers in the water. Practice good etiquette and avoid collisions by communicating with others and giving them plenty of space.

Surfing Etiquette

Surfing etiquette refers to behavior in the water among surfers. It includes a set of guidelines that ensure the safety of surfers and the preservation of the surfing environment.

Avoid accidents and conflicts in the water, especially in crowded surf spots. Surfing etiquette is based on respect for other surfers and the local culture.

Following surfing etiquette not only shows respect for fellow surfers but also enhances the surfing experience for everyone. It helps maintain a positive and friendly atmosphere in the water and ensures that everyone has a fair chance to catch waves.

Rules of the Water

The idea of surfing paints a picture of fun. The word "rules," on the other hand, has a negative connotation.

Well, rules in surfing exist because surfing is an activity that involves multiple people sharing a limited space in the water. Without rules, the risk of accidents and collisions increases, which can lead to injuries and conflicts between surfers.

Their purpose? Create a safe and enjoyable experience for all surfers!

By following rules, surfers can avoid dangerous situations and ensure that everyone has a fair opportunity to catch waves. This promotes a positive and friendly atmosphere in the water and enhances the surfing experience for all participants. However, strong localism exits at some local surf spots and non-locals are usually not welcomed. Ask someone local to avoid those areas.

Right-of-Way Rules

These rules refer to the guidelines that determine who has priority to catch a wave when multiple surfers are attempting to catch it. Following these rules ensures that surfers can safely and efficiently navigate the water without collisions or conflicts.

The basic principle of these rules is that the surfer who is closest to the peak of the wave has priority over other surfers. The surfer in the optimal position has the best chance of catching the wave and should be given priority to do so.

If a surfer is already riding a wave, other surfers should not attempt to drop in on them or interfere with their ride.

Here are some of the right-of-way rules followed by surfers:

- **The surfer closest to the peak of the wave has priority:** When multiple surfers are paddling for the same wave, the surfer who is closest to the breaking part of the wave has the right of way.

- **The first surfer up has priority:** When two surfers catch the same wave at the same time, the surfer who stands up and catches the wave first has priority.

- **The inside surfer has priority:** If two surfers are on different sections of the wave, the surfer who is closest to the breaking part of the wave has priority.

- **Yield to the surfer already riding the wave:** If a surfer is already riding the wave, other surfers should not attempt to drop in on them or interfere with their ride.

- **Avoid collisions:** It is the responsibility of every

surfer to avoid collisions with others. If a surfer sees another surfer heading their way, they should paddle in a different direction to avoid a collision.

Advanced SUP Surfing

Advanced SUP surfing requires a high level of skill, balance, and experience. Learn the basic skills first, and don't fast-forward to this level.

Without a high skill level, attempting advanced SUP surfing techniques can be dangerous and lead to injury. It's vital to progress gradually and seek proper instruction.

To take your SUP surfing to the next level, consider the following tips:

- **Master the basics:** Before attempting advanced maneuvers, make sure you have a solid foundation in basic SUP surfing techniques, including paddling, turning, and catching waves.

- **Choose the right board:** Advanced SUP surfers typically use shorter, narrower boards that are more maneuverable and responsive to their movements.

- **Surf and surf some more!:** The key to mastering advanced SUP surfing is practice. Spend as much time as possible on the water, and don't be afraid to try new maneuvers and techniques.

- **Learn to read the waves:** Advanced SUP surfers must be able to anticipate and respond to changing wave conditions, including the size, shape, and direction of waves.

- **Experiment with different maneuvers:** Once you have a solid foundation in basic techniques, try experimenting with more advanced maneuvers, such as bottom turns, top turns, and cutbacks.

Advanced Techniques

Learning advanced SUP surfing techniques can be a wild ride for enthusiasts who want to take their skills to the next level.

It allows for more challenging waves and maneuvers, improving overall physical fitness and mental focus. The feeling of successfully executing a new technique can be incredibly satisfying and fuels the desire to continue pushing boundaries and learning more.

Try these techniques to build your SUP surfing skills:

- **Rail control:** Use your feet and knees to control the rails of your board, allowing you to make quick turns and maneuvers on the wave face. Practice shifting your weight to adjust the angle of your board.

- **Bottom turns:** Mastering the bottom turn is key to carving up the wave face. As you approach the bottom of the wave, drop your back hand to initiate the turn and use your paddle for added stability and control.

- **Top turns:** Once you've mastered the bottom turn, the top turn is your next challenge. As you approach the top of the wave, shift your weight forward and pivot on the tail of your board to carve back down the wave face.

- **Cutback:** A cutback is a sharp turn that allows you to change direction quickly while still riding the wave. To execute a cutback, turn the board sharply towards the wave's breaking lip and then quickly shift your weight back towards the tail to complete the turn.

- **Floater:** A floater is a maneuver where you ride up and over the breaking section of the wave instead of cutting back or bottom turning.

To execute a floater, generate speed as you approach the breaking section of the wave, then shift your weight forward as you ride up and over the wave. Use your paddle to maintain your balance as you come back down the face of the wave.

Basic Etiquette Tips for Beginners

If you're a beginner in surfing, familiarize yourself with basic surfing etiquette. Surfing etiquette is a set of unwritten rules that all surfers should follow to ensure everyone's safety and enjoyment in the water.

Here are some etiquette tips for beginners:

- **Learn the local rules and customs:** Every surfing spot has its own set of rules and customs. Take time to research and learn about them before paddling out.

- **Start in beginner-friendly areas:** Choose beginner-friendly spots with small, easy-to-ride waves and a lower number of surfers. This will help you gain confidence and experience without getting in the way of more experienced surfers.

- **Observe before joining in:** Take time to observe the behavior of other surfers, the wave patterns, and the water conditions before paddling out. This will help you to avoid dangerous situations and to better understand the dynamics of the surf spot.

- **Don't drop in:** Always wait your turn to catch a wave, and never drop in on another surfer who is already riding a wave. This is not only a safety concern but also considered disrespectful.

Etiquette in Crowded Surf Spots

Crowded surf spots can be challenging for even the most experienced surfers. When surfing in crowded areas, it's essential to be mindful of others and practice good etiquette to ensure a safe and enjoyable experience for everyone.

Here are some etiquette tips for surfing in crowded areas:

- **Navigating crowds:** Be aware of your surroundings and the behavior of other surfers. Try to avoid getting in the way of others, and always look before taking off on a wave.

- **Being patient and respectful:** It can be frustrating to wait for a wave in a crowded lineup, but it's essential to be patient and respectful of others. Don't drop in on other surfers or snake waves; wait your turn to catch a wave.

- **Avoiding bad behavior:** Surfing in crowded areas can bring out bad behavior in some surfers, but it's important to maintain a positive attitude and avoid engaging in aggressive or disrespectful behavior. Remember that everyone is there to have fun and enjoy the waves.

- **Communicating with others:** Communication is key in crowded lineups. Use hand signals and vocal cues to let other surfers know your intentions and to avoid collisions.

- **Giving space:** Try to leave enough space between yourself and other surfers to avoid collisions or interfering with each other's rides. Don't crowd the peak or paddle inside of others.

Forecasts, Tides and Conditions

Understanding forecasts, tides, and conditions is a high-value skill. It allows surfers to formulate sound decisions, stay safe, and maximize their odds of catching the best waves possible while respecting the environment.

Surf Forecasts

Surf forecasts are predictions of wave and weather conditions at a particular surf spot. These forecasts typically include information about wave height, swell direction, wind speed and direction, tide times, and water temperature. Understanding how to read and interpret surf forecasts is essential for any surfer looking to catch waves safely and effectively.

Here are some tips for reading and interpreting surf forecasts:

- **Know the terms:** Familiarize yourself with the terminology used in surf forecasts. For example, swell direction refers to the direction from which the swell is coming, while wind speed and direction describe the speed and direction of the wind.

- **Understand the numbers:** Surf forecasts typically include numerical data that describes wave height, swell period, and wind speed. For example, a forecast might predict 4-6 foot waves with a 10-second swell period and 10-knot winds.

- **Use visual aids:** Many surf forecasts include visual aids, such as charts or graphs, to help surfers better understand the information being presented.

- **Check multiple sources:** Surf forecasts can vary from one source to another, so it's a good idea to check multiple forecasts and compare the information to get a more accurate picture of the surf conditions.

- **Consider local knowledge:** While surf forecasts can be a useful tool, they don't always paint a complete picture of the surf conditions at a particular spot. Local knowledge, such as knowledge of tide times and the impact of the wind on a particular break, can be invaluable for predicting surf conditions.

Tides

Tides are the rise and fall of sea levels caused by the gravitational pull of the moon and the sun on the Earth's oceans. Understanding tides is important for surfers because they can have a significant impact on surfing conditions.

Here's how tides affect surfing conditions:

- **Wave height:** The height of waves can vary significantly depending on the tide. Generally, waves are smaller at low tide and larger at high tide. This is because as the tide rises, it covers more of the reef or sandbar, causing the wave to break closer to the shore and creating a steeper face.

- **Wave shape:** The shape of waves can also change depending on the tide. At low tide, waves may break in a shallow, fast, and hollow manner, while at high tide, waves may break in a slower, more mellow manner.

- **Water depth:** Tides can affect the depth of the water, which in turn can affect the behavior of the waves.

For example, as the tide rises, the water may become deeper, allowing waves to break more smoothly and with less power. Conversely, as the tide drops, the water may become shallower, causing waves to break more erratically and with more power.

- **Currents:** Tides can also affect the currents in the water, which can impact the behavior of the waves and the safety of the surfer. For example, at low tide, there may be stronger currents and rip currents, which can make it more difficult for a surfer to paddle out or to stay in position.

Surfing Conditions

Surfing conditions refer to the combination of factors that impact the quality of the waves and the overall experience for the surfer. There are several factors that affect surfing conditions, including wind, swell, tide, and water temperature.

Here's a breakdown of how wind, swell, and tide can impact surfing conditions:

- **Wind:** Wind plays a significant role in shaping the waves and creating the conditions for surfing. When the wind blows offshore–blowing out to sea–it helps create clean, well-formed waves ideal for surfing.

  Conversely, when the wind blows onshore–blowing towards the shore–it can create choppy, messy waves that are difficult to ride.

- **Swell:** Swell refers to the size and frequency of the waves. The height of the waves is determined by the strength of the wind and the distance over which it blows. The frequency of the waves is determined by the amount of time between each wave. Generally, bigger and more frequent waves are better for surfing.

- **Tide:** As discussed earlier, the tide can have a significant impact on the behavior of the waves. The state of the tide, whether it is high tide or low tide, can affect the shape, size, and power of the waves.

Fun Fact

Did you know that SUP surfing can be more relaxing?

SUP offers a unique viewpoint, whether cruising on calm waters or riding waves in the ocean and lets let you observe marine life and the surrounding environment without being too intrusive.

With little impact on the environment, SUP allows for a memorable and sustainable way to appreciate the beauty of nature.

Chapter 6: SUP Foil

Foiling is like flying above the water. Think of it like a bird soaring effortlessly in the sky with its wings.

Like that bird, a foiler glides above the water with the help of a hydrofoil attached to the bottom of the board. The foil lifts the board out of the water, reducing drag and allowing for a smooth, fast, and exhilarating ride.

It's a sensation unlike any other—as if you're hovering over the water's surface like a magic carpet.

Foiling has become popular among water sports enthusiasts due to the unique experience it provides and the ability to ride waves in an exciting way.

Don't know the first thing about foiling?

I'll help you.

In this chapter, we'll talk about foiling—the experience of foiling, foiling techniques, thoughts on foiling, and more. And, because foiling is promising, we'll also discuss its future.

What Is Foiling?

Foiling, also known as hydrofoiling, is a technology that allows a surfboard or a SUP board to lift off the water's surface and ride on a hydrofoil.

A hydrofoil is a wing-like structure that extends from the bottom of the board and lifts it out of the water as it gains speed. This creates less drag and allows for higher speeds and smoother rides.

In the context of SUP, a foil board is typically short with a mast and hydrofoil attached underneath. The rider stands on the board and uses a paddle to propel themselves forward.

The Experience of Foiling

The experience of foiling is unlike any other form of water sports.

Riding a hydrofoil board, whether it's SUP foiling, kite foiling, wing foiling, or foil surfing provides a unique sensation of flying over the water's surface. The feeling is often described as weightless and almost ethereal, as though you're hovering over the water like a bird in flight.

At first, getting up on the hydrofoil can be a challenge, as it requires a combination of balance, coordination, and speed. But once you're up and riding, the feeling is truly exhilarating. The hydrofoil creates lift by generating an upward force that lifts the board and rider out of the water, allowing them to glide smoothly over the surface.

As the hydrofoil reduces drag and resistance, riders can achieve faster speeds than they would on a traditional surfboard or SUP board. The feeling of speed combined with the sensation of floating above the water creates a thrilling rush that is hard to replicate with any other water sport.

Riding a hydrofoil also requires a high degree of focus and concentration, as even the slightest shift in weight or movement can significantly impact the board's trajectory. It's a challenge that requires a combination of physical skill and mental agility, making it an incredibly rewarding and satisfying experience for those who master it.

Foiling Techniques

There are several different techniques used in foiling, each with its own unique challenges and benefits.

The discussions below will cover these techniques.

Pumping

Pumping on a hydrofoil board is an essential skill that offers several benefits to riders. The most significant advantage of pumping is that it allows riders to maintain their speed and momentum without relying on external forces such as wind or waves.

This means that riders can cover more distance and stay on the water for longer periods, making the most of their hydrofoil session.

Pumping also offers a low-impact workout that can improve overall fitness, core stability, and balance. As riders use their legs to generate the pumping motion, it can also improve leg strength and endurance.

Pumping can help riders navigate through areas with less wind or smaller waves, making it a versatile skill that can enhance the overall hydrofoil experience. With regular practice and dedication, pumping can become a smooth and effortless motion that adds a new level of fun and excitement to your hydrofoil sessions.

Here's a step-by-step guide on how to pump on a hydrofoil board without foot straps:

1. **Monitor water conditions:** Pumping on a hydrofoil board requires calm or flat water. Make sure to find a calm and safe area to practice pumping.

2. **Position yourself on the board:** Stand on the board with your feet slightly apart and your front foot near the front of the board. Your knees should be slightly bent, and your weight should be evenly distributed between your feet.

3. **Generate lift:** Start by pressing down firmly on your back foot while pulling up with your front foot. This motion should generate lift and create a small hop in the board.

4. **Shift your weight:** As the board lifts out of the water, shift your weight forward and use your front foot to guide the board back down into the water.

5. **Repeat the motion:** Continue to repeat the pumping motion, shifting your weight from your back foot to your front foot and using the lift generated by the foil to propel the board forward.

6. **Maintain speed and control:** Once you have built up enough speed, you can maintain it by pumping consistently and using the lift generated by the foil to maintain your speed and stability.

7. **Persevere:** Pumping on a hydrofoil board requires commitment, practice, and patience. Don't get discouraged if you don't get it right away, keep practicing, and you'll soon master the art of pumping on a hydrofoil board.

Carving

Carving on a hydrofoil board is a challenging skill that requires practice and dedication to master. It involves shifting your weight on your front foot or back foot, allowing the foil to curve through the water and create a smooth, flowing turn.

To carve effectively, the rider must maintain a proper balance, weight distribution, and body position while adjusting the angle of the foil with subtle movements. The speed and direction of the turn also require precise control, which can be difficult to achieve without proper technique and experience.

However, once you start to master the art of carving, it can add a new level of excitement and creativity to your hydrofoil experience. Carving allows you to explore new lines, create dynamic turns, and push the boundaries of what's possible on a hydrofoil board. While challenging, carving is a rewarding skill to master and can take your hydrofoil experience to the next level.

Here is a step-by-step guide on how to carve on a hydrofoil board:

1. **Start by riding straight:** Before you can carve, you need to be comfortable riding straight on your hydrofoil board. Make sure you have good balance and control before attempting to carve.

2. **Shift your weight:** To initiate a carve, shift your weight to your heels or toes, depending on which direction you want to turn.

3. **Angle your foil:** As you shift your weight, angle your foil in the direction you want to turn. This will help to create a more aggressive turn and maintain your speed.

4. **Use your body to control the turn:** As you carve, use your body to control the turn. Lean into the turn with your shoulders and hips, and use your arms to help guide the board in the direction you want to go.

5. **Keep your eyes on the horizon:** As you carve, it's important to keep your eyes on the horizon. This will help you maintain your balance and control and ensure that you stay on course.

6. **Release the turn:** When ready to release the turn, shift your weight back to the center and straighten out your foil.

7. **Keep doing it:** Carving on a hydrofoil board takes practice. Don't get discouraged if you don't get it right away, keep practicing, and you'll soon master the art of carving on a hydrofoil board.

Downwind Foiling

Downwind foiling is a thrilling and challenging form of foiling that involves riding the hydrofoil board downwind, using the power of the wind to generate speed and lift.

This type of foiling requires a combination of skill, experience, and the right conditions to achieve maximum speed and performance.

Here's a step-by-step guide on how to downwind foil:

1. **Choose the right conditions:** Downwind foiling requires a combination of wind and waves to create the perfect conditions. Look for a day with consistent wind speeds of at least 15 knots and a moderate swell. Make sure to choose a downwind route that is suitable for your skill level.

2. **Rig up:** Before hitting the water, make sure you have all the necessary gear. This includes a foil board, a foil, a paddle, and a wetsuit or appropriate clothing for the conditions.

3. **Launch and get up to speed:** Start paddling or pedaling your board to get up to speed. Once you reach a speed of around 7-8 knots, you can start to lift your foil out of the water and ride on the hydrofoil.

4. **Use the wind and waves to your advantage:** As you ride downwind, use the wind and waves to your advantage. Position yourself in the sweet spot between the wind and the waves to maintain your speed and stability.

5. **Adjust your body position:** To maintain balance and control, adjust your body position as you ride. Keep your weight centered over the board and make subtle adjustments to your posture to maintain your trajectory.

6. **Keep your eyes ahead:** As you ride, keep your eyes focused on the horizon ahead of you. This will help you anticipate changes in the wind and waves and adjust your course accordingly.

7. **Plan your exit:** As you approach the end of your downwind run, plan your exit carefully. Look for a safe spot to bring your foil back down to the water, and use your paddle to slow your speed and maintain control.

8. **Repeat:** With practice and experience, you'll be able to master the art of downwind foiling and enjoy the thrill of riding on the hydrofoil.

Fun Fact

Strapless is the most comfortable riding stance. It provides the freedom of changing your stance without using foot straps but requires practice.

This technique requires good balance and body positioning, as well as a deep understanding of how the hydrofoil responds to different movements and weight shifts.

Foiling and Its Challenges

Foiling in crowded lineups can pose potential hazards to the foiler and other paddlers, surfers, and anyone in the water.

Foiling requires high speeds and sharp turns, making it difficult for other surfers or paddlers to avoid foilers or for foilers to avoid objects in the water. The long, pointed foil also poses a risk of serious injury to anyone it comes into contact with.

Plus, the speed and unpredictability of foiling can disrupt the established flow of a lineup, leading to tension and conflict among surfers. As such, it is important for foilers to exercise caution and respect for others in crowded surfing areas.

Some of the risks associated with foiling include collisions with other watercraft, injuries from falls, and damage to the foil equipment. Here are some tips on how to avoid these potential hazards:

- **Choose your foiling location wisely:** Look for areas with fewer crowds and less boat traffic. Crowded lineups can be dangerous as there's a greater risk of collisions.

- **Be vigilant:** Always keep an eye out for other watercraft in the area and stay alert for potential hazards.

- **Use protective gear:** Wearing a helmet and impact vest can reduce the risk of injury in the event of a fall or collision.

- **Know your limits:** Foiling can be physically demanding and requires a high level of skill. Don't attempt to foil in conditions that exceed your ability level.

- **Respect others in the water:** Be aware of the surf etiquette in your area and respect the rights of others in the water. Don't hog the waves or endanger others by flying too close to them.

Benefits of Foiling

Before hitting the water, spend some time visualizing yourself riding a wave on your foil board. Visualizing your movements and anticipating the flow of the water can help you make quicker, more intuitive decisions while foiling.

According to Closier (2020), the feeling is nothing short of amazing, and you may want to visualize it.

You can also practice visualization techniques while on land to improve your mental focus and prepare yourself for a successful ride.

Want more tips?

Here are ways you can make the most of your time on your foil:

- **Wing foil:** Instead of using a paddle, you can use a wing while foiling. If you are interested in it, reach out to experts in this sport.

    Wing foiling or wing surfing has become a popular water sport as an alternative to windsurfing or kiteboarding (or kitesurfing) due to less complexity in terms of required equipment and skill set.

- **Kite foil:** You can also use a kite while foiling. Kiteboarding is another popular water sport, and it can be done using a foil board.

    However, kiteboarding requires whole different skills other than foiling techniques. Seek exports in this sport and take lessons before jumping into it.

    You will be an expert in using foil boards if you know how to do those foiling variations.

Thoughts from the Surfing Community

Foiling has brought significant changes to the lineup, particularly in the way it has impacted the relationship between surfers and SUP paddlers.

A Negative Outlook

Initially, foiling was met with resistance from the surfing community, much like SUP when it first gained popularity.

Let's name the reasons for the resistance.

- **Perception of SUP as a beginner's sport:** Surfing has a long history and culture that values skill, experience, and respect for the ocean. There is a perception that SUP foiling somehow disregards that.

- **Potential for creating hazards in crowded lineups:** It reels in more participants. With more people in the lineup, comes a greater potential for accidents and injuries.

- **Disrupting the flow of the lineup:** Surfing has an unspoken etiquette that governs the way surfers share the waves. Some surfers felt that SUP foilers disrupted the established flow of the lineup—and created tension.

Positive Vibes

Despite initial resistance from the surfing community, SUP foiling has gained a strong following and positive outlook. Many see it as an exciting and innovative way to enjoy the ocean and push the limits of their surfing skills.

With advancements in technology and safety measures, concerns about hazards and disruptions in crowded lineups are being addressed. Ultimately, a positive attitude towards SUP foiling can bring new excitement to the sport of surfing.

The Impact of Foiling on the SUP Community

Foiling is a relatively recent development in water sports that has had a significant impact on the surfing and SUP communities. The emergence of foiling has created a new dynamic in the lineup, forcing surfers and SUP paddlers to coexist and share waves in ways that were previously unheard of.

Foiling has changed the way people approach the lineup, with foilers often taking off on waves that surfers would have overlooked. This has created a new layer of competition in the lineup, as surfers and foilers vie for the same waves, sometimes even riding them together.

As a result, this forced surfers and SUP paddlers to communicate more effectively in the water, establishing a new level of mutual respect and cooperation.

The emergence of foiling has also changed the perception of SUP in the surfing community.

Initially seen as a sport for beginners or tourists, the addition of foiling has elevated SUP to a new level of athleticism and excitement. Foiling has brought new possibilities to SUP, allowing paddlers to ride waves that were previously inaccessible and to experiment with new techniques and maneuvers.

The New Normal: Surfers, Paddlers, and Foilers Sharing the Lineup

Today, the lineup has evolved into a dynamic and diverse community where surfers, paddlers, and foilers coexist in a spirit of mutual respect and cooperation.

What was once a source of tension and resistance has now become an opportunity for growth and exploration as people from different backgrounds and disciplines come together to share their love of the ocean.

This diversity of disciplines has created a vibrant and inclusive lineup where people of all skill levels and backgrounds can come together to share their love of the ocean.

Beginners and experts alike now have the opportunity to learn from each other, with experienced surfers and foilers providing guidance and support to those who are just starting out.

For the most part, this has created a sense of community in the lineup, where people are eager to share their knowledge and passion for the ocean with others.

Here are a few examples of how surfers, paddlers, and foilers have come together to form a cohesive community in the lineup:

- **Surf schools offer SUP and foiling lessons:** Many surf schools now offer lessons for SUP and foiling and teach both surfing and SUP techniques.

  This has helped to break down the barriers among the sports and has encouraged people to try their individual disciplines, fostering a sense of community among participants.

- **Joint events and competitions:** Many surfing competitions now include SUP and foiling divisions, encouraging athletes from different disciplines to compete and learn from each other.

  These events provide an opportunity for surfers, paddlers, and foilers to come together in a shared space, building connections and fostering a sense of camaraderie.

- **Environmental activism and community outreach:** Many surfers, paddlers, and foilers share a deep love and respect for the ocean and have organized community events and environmental activism campaigns to protect and preserve it.

  By working together towards a common goal, these individuals have built strong bonds and have forged a sense of community that transcends their individual disciplines.

- **Informal gatherings and social events:** In many coastal communities, surfers, paddlers, and foilers can be found hanging out together, sharing stories and experiences over food and drinks.

  These informal gatherings provide an opportunity for people to connect on a personal level, building relationships that extend beyond the lineup and into everyday life.

The Future Looks Bright

Looking ahead to the future, there is reason to be hopeful about the place of SUP in the surfing lineup. With each passing year, more and more people are discovering the joy and excitement of SUP and foiling and are eager to explore the ocean in new and innovative ways.

As the lineup continues to evolve and diversify, there will inevitably be challenges and conflicts along the way; however, by building on the spirit of cooperation and respect that has already been established, surfers, paddlers, and foilers can work together to create a more inclusive and welcoming environment for all.

With continued innovation and experimentation, there is no limit to what surfers, paddlers, and foilers can achieve together.

By embracing new technologies and approaches and by continuing to build connections and relationships within the community, we can look forward to a future where the ocean is a place of unity and shared joy rather than division and conflict.

Chapter 7: SUP Yoga and Workout

In recent years, SUP has seen an exponential rise in popularity, and it's easy to see why. Not only does it offer an excellent way to enjoy the great outdoors, but it also provides numerous physical and mental health benefits. But that's not all!

With the advent of SUP yoga and workouts, the benefits are amplified. Combining SUP with yoga and a workout provides a full body workout and promotes mental relaxation, ultimately resulting in enhanced physical and mental well-being.

So why not take advantage of this fantastic combination?

In this chapter, we will explore how SUP can be combined with yoga and working out. We'll discuss how it at least doubles the physical and mental benefits, the calories you can burn, specific yoga poses, workout routines, and more.

How Many Calories Can You Burn?

According to research (Cox, 2023), you can burn calories with SUP. If you need to lose weight and love being in the water at the same time, why not consider SUP yoga and workout?

The number of calories burned during a SUP yoga and workout session depends on a variety of factors, including body weight, the intensity of the workout, and the duration of the activity.

On average, it is estimated that an hour of moderate-intensity SUP activity can burn between 500 to 700 calories.

However, calorie burn can vary widely depending on individual factors and the intensity of the workout. You need to listen to your body and not focus solely on the number of calories burned.

Benefits of SUP Yoga and Workout

SUP yoga challenges balance, stability, and core strength, while a SUP workout engages all major muscle groups.

What can SUP yoga and workouts do for you?

- **Improved balance and stability:** SUP requires good balance. It challenges and improves balance skills, helping individuals develop better overall balance and stability, which can benefit other activities and prevent falls.

- **Increased activation of deep stabilizing muscles:** Balancing on the board activates the deep stabilizing muscles in the core, legs, and feet. These muscles are often neglected in traditional workouts, leading to imbalances and weaknesses.

- **Improved strength, posture, and toning:** SUP yoga and workouts engage all major muscle groups, improving overall strength and toning the body. Additionally, the focus on balance and alignment helps improve posture.

- **Mental benefits, such as stress reduction and relaxation:** Being on the water and practicing yoga or exercising outdoors can reduce stress and promote relaxation. The sounds and sights of nature can have a calming effect on the mind.

- **A low-impact workout that is easy on the joints:** SUP yoga and workouts are low-impact activities that are gentle on the joints. This makes it a great option for individuals who want to exercise without putting too much stress on their joints.

- **An enjoyable and fun way to exercise:** SUP yoga and workouts are enjoyable activities that can make exercise feel less like a chore. This can make it easier to stay consistent with a fitness routine.

- **The ability to connect with nature and enjoy the outdoors:** Being on the water and in nature can promote feelings of well-being and connection to the environment.

Getting Started With SUP Yoga and Workout

Getting started with SUP yoga and workouts is relatively easy and requires minimal equipment.

The best way to get started is to find a reputable instructor and begin with basic classes to develop proper technique and safety.

Beginners should also start on calm and flat water to develop balance and confidence before progressing to more challenging conditions.

Helpful Item

Invest in quality equipment that fits your needs and budget. Renting equipment is also an option for those who want to try SUP yoga and workouts before investing in their own equipment.

Apart from a paddleboard, you may need this:

- **Anchor:** An anchor can be used to keep the board in place during a SUP Yoga or workout session. It's important to choose an anchor that is appropriate for the size and weight of the board.

Location: A Safe and Calm Space

Finding the right location for SUP yoga and workout depends on individual preferences and skill levels.

Consider these factors when searching for a suitable location:

- **Calm water:** SUP yoga and SUP workout require stability and balance, which can be challenging in choppy or rough waters. Look for locations with calm waters, such as lakes, bays, or calm sections of rivers or oceans.

- **Accessible shorelines:** Look for locations with easy access to the shoreline, such as boat ramps or beaches. It's important to consider the distance between the parking area and the water, as carrying a heavy board and equipment can be tiring.

- **Scenery:** SUP yoga and workout can be a great way to connect with nature and enjoy the scenery. Look for locations with beautiful views, such as mountains, forests, or wildlife.

- **Regulations:** Some bodies of water may have regulations regarding the use of paddleboards, such as permits or restrictions on the use of anchors or leashes. It's important to research and follow the regulations of the location.

- **Safety:** Consider the safety of the location, such as the presence of hazards like rocks or submerged objects, strong currents or winds, and the availability of rescue services in case of emergencies.

- **Crowds:** SUP yoga and workout can be a peaceful and calming experience, but crowded locations can be noisy and distracting. Look for locations with fewer crowds or times when the location is less busy.

Tips (Especially for Beginners)

By starting with basic poses and focusing on their breath, beginners can build a solid foundation for SUP yoga and workout. It's important to take it slow, be patient, and prioritize safety at all times.

How to start:

- **Start with basic poses:** Begin with basic yoga poses that are easy to perform on a paddleboard, such as downward-facing dog, child's pose, or seated twists. As balance and stability improve, more advanced poses can be added.
- **Focus on breathing:** Breath control is an essential component of yoga and can help individuals stay focused and calm on the water. Focus on deep, steady breaths, and try to sync the breath with the movements.
- **Keep a low center of gravity:** Maintain a low center of gravity by engaging the core and keeping the hips stable. This can improve balance and stability on the water.
- **Use the paddle for support:** The paddle can be used as a support prop during poses, especially for balancing poses. It can be placed in the water to provide stability and support.
- **Take breaks:** SUP yoga and workout can be challenging, both physically and mentally. It's important to take breaks and rest when needed.

SUP Yoga Poses

SUP Yoga poses are practiced on a paddleboard on the water, which adds an additional level of challenge and requires the use of muscles that may not be engaged during traditional yoga on land.

Basic Poses

Basic poses in SUP yoga can help establish balance and stability on the paddleboard. They're great for beginners and for those having trouble with their balance.

Here are some basic poses that can be practiced on a paddleboard:

- **Mountain Pose:** This pose helps to improve balance and stability. Stand with your feet hip-distance apart on the paddleboard, with your toes pointing forward and your arms at your sides. Engage your core, lengthen your spine, and lift the crown of your head towards the sky. Breathe deeply and hold the pose for several breaths.

- **Downward-Facing Dog:** This pose helps to stretch the hamstrings, calves, and spine while also building upper body strength. Start on your hands and knees on the paddleboard, with your hands shoulder-width apart and your knees hip-width apart.

  Lift your hips up and back, straightening your arms and legs to create an inverted V-shape with your body. Keep your head and neck relaxed, and breathe deeply.

- **Child's Pose:** This pose helps to release tension in the lower back and hips. Start on your hands and knees on the paddleboard, with your toes touching and your knees wider than hip-distance apart.

  Sit back onto your heels and stretch your arms forward, resting your forehead on the paddleboard. Breathe deeply and hold the pose for several breaths.

- **Warrior I:** This pose helps to build strength in the legs and core while also improving balance. Stand at the center of the board with your feet hip-width apart, then step your right foot forward and turn your left foot out to a 45-degree angle.

  Bend your right knee to a 90-degree angle and raise your arms overhead, with your palms facing each other. Breathe deeply and hold the pose for several breaths before switching sides.

- **Tree Pose:** This pose helps to improve balance and strengthen the legs. Start in Mountain Pose, then shift your weight onto your left foot and lift your right foot off the board.

Place the sole of your right foot against the inside of your left thigh, with your toes pointing towards the ground. Bring your hands to your heart center and breathe deeply. Hold the pose for several breaths before switching sides.

Intermediate Poses

Intermediate poses in SUP yoga can help raise the bar in terms of strength, balance, and flexibility. They're ideal for the more experienced paddlers.

Here are some intermediate poses that can be practiced on a paddleboard:

- **Warrior Pose:** This pose helps to strengthen the legs and core while also improving balance. Start in Mountain Pose, then step your right foot forward and turn your left foot out to a 90-degree angle.

Bend your right knee to a 90-degree angle and extend your arms out to the sides, with your palms facing down. Breathe deeply and hold the pose for several breaths before switching sides.

- **Plank Pose:** This pose helps to strengthen the arms, core, and back while also improving balance. Start on your hands and knees on the paddleboard, then step your feet back to come into a plank position, with your shoulders directly over your wrists and your body in a straight line from head to heels.

Hold the pose for several breaths before lowering back down to your hands and knees.

- **Boat Pose:** This pose helps to strengthen the core and improve balance. Sit on the paddleboard with your knees bent and your feet flat on the board.

  Lean back slightly and lift your feet off the board, straightening your legs to a 45-degree angle. Reach your arms forward, parallel to the board, and breathe deeply. Hold the pose for several breaths before lowering back down.

- **Side Plank:** This pose strengthens the arms, obliques, and legs while improving balance. Start in plank position, then shift your weight onto your left hand and the outer edge of your left foot, stacking your right foot on top of the left.

  Extend your right arm up towards the sky and hold the pose for several breaths before switching sides.

- **Upward-Facing Dog:** This pose strengthens the arms, shoulders, and back while improving posture.

  Start lying face-down on the paddleboard, then press into your hands and lift your chest, keeping your legs extended behind you. Keep your shoulders relaxed and breathe deeply as you hold the pose for several breaths.

Advanced Poses

Advanced SUP yoga poses require a strong foundation of basic and intermediate poses, as well as experience and confidence on the paddleboard.

Here are advanced poses that you can do on a paddleboard:

- **Headstand:** This pose strengthens the upper body and improves balance, focus, and concentration. Start in a kneeling position on the board and place your forearms on the board with your palms facing down.

Clasp your hands together and place the crown of your head on the board. Straighten your legs and walk your feet towards your head, lifting your hips up towards the sky. Hold the pose for several breaths before lowering back down.

- **Handstand:** This pose strengthens the upper body and improves balance, focus, and confidence. Start in downward-facing dog pose, then walk your feet towards your hands and lift one leg up towards the sky.

  Hop off of the other foot and lift both legs up into a handstand, pressing your palms firmly into the board. Hold the pose for several breaths before lowering back down.

- **Scorpion Pose:** This pose strengthens the upper body and improves flexibility and balance. Start in downward-facing dog pose, then lift one leg up towards the sky and bend your knee, bringing your heel towards your head.

  Lower your head towards the board and reach your foot towards your head, bending your elbows and lifting your chest towards the sky. Hold the pose for several breaths before switching sides.

- **Camel Pose:** This pose improves posture and back flexibility. Start in a kneeling position on the board and bring your hands to your lower back.

  Press your hips forward and lift your chest towards the sky, keeping your gaze upwards. Hold the pose for several breaths before lowering back down.

- **Wheel Pose:** This pose strengthens the arms, shoulders, and back while improving flexibility and balance. Start lying on your back on the board with your knees bent and your feet flat.

Bring your hands to the board beside your ears and press into your hands and feet, lifting your hips and chest up towards the sky. Hold the pose for several breaths before lowering back down.

SUP Yoga Sequence

A SUP yoga sequence can be customized to suit individual needs and preferences.

Here is an example of sequence worth trying:

- **Sun Salutations:** Start in mountain pose on the board and raise your arms overhead, then fold forward into a standing forward bend. Step back into plank pose and lower down to low plank pose, then lift into upward-facing dog.

  From there, lift your hips back into downward-facing dog pose and hold for several breaths before returning to mountain pose.

- **Warrior Series:** From mountain pose, step one foot back and lower into a lunge, with your front knee bent and your back leg straight. Raise your arms overhead and hold for several breaths before switching sides.

  Repeat on both sides, then move on to warrior II pose by turning your back foot perpendicular to the board and extending your arms out to the sides.

- **Balancing Poses:** Balancing poses, such as tree pose and eagle pose, can be challenging on a paddleboard but are great for improving focus and stability. To practice tree pose, stand with one foot firmly on the board and bring the sole of your other foot to rest against your inner thigh.

Bring your hands to your heart center and hold for several breaths before switching sides. To practice the eagle pose, cross one leg over the other and wrap your opposite arm under the other arm. Lift your elbows and bring your hands together in front of your face. Hold for several breaths before switching sides.

SUP Workout

A SUP workout can be a great way to improve your fitness and overall health while enjoying the outdoors.

Here are some tips and ideas for a challenging and effective SUP workout:

- **Warm-up:** Before starting your workout, take a few minutes to warm up your muscles with some light paddling or yoga stretches. This will help prevent injuries and prepare your body for the workout ahead.
- **Cardio:** Paddling is a great form of cardio and can be made more challenging by increasing your speed or adding intervals of high-intensity paddling. Try to maintain a steady pace and keep your heart rate up for at least 20-30 minutes.
- **Strength training:** Paddleboarding provides an opportunity to work on your upper body strength. Paddling itself is a great workout for your arms, shoulders, and back, but you can also incorporate other exercises such as push-ups, plank variations, and even bicep curls using resistance bands.
- **Core stability:** Paddleboarding requires a lot of core stability and can be a great way to work on your abs and back muscles. Try incorporating exercises such as sit-ups, Russian twists, and plank variations into your workout.

- **Cool-down:** After your workout, take a few minutes to cool down and stretch your muscles. This will help prevent soreness and improve your flexibility over time.

SUP Workout Routine

Incorporating SUP into your existing workout routine provides a low-impact full-body workout. Being on the water and surrounded by nature can also have a meditative effect.

Don't have a routine yet?

Here are routines you may be interested in:

Routine 1:
- Warm-up: 5 minutes of easy paddling
- Paddle sprints: 5 sets of 1 minute sprints, with 30 seconds of rest in between
- Squats: 3 sets of 12 reps, using the paddle as a weight
- Lunges: 3 sets of 12 reps on each leg, using the paddle as a weight
- Push-ups: 3 sets of 10 reps, with your hands on the paddle for added stability
- Planks: 3 sets of 30 seconds each

Routine 2:
- Warm-up: 5 minutes of easy paddling
- Paddle sprints: 3 sets of 2 minutes sprints, with 1 minute of rest in between
- Squats: 3 sets of 15 reps, using the paddle as a weight
- Lunges: 3 sets of 15 reps on each leg, using the paddle as a weight

- Push-ups: 3 sets of 12 reps, with your hands on the paddle for added stability
- Planks: 3 sets of 45 seconds each

Routine 3:
- Warm-up: 5 minutes of easy paddling
- Paddle sprints: 4 sets of 30 seconds sprints, with 15 seconds of rest in between
- Squats: 3 sets of 20 reps, using the paddle as a weight
- Lunges: 3 sets of 20 reps on each leg, using the paddle as a weight
- Push-ups: 3 sets of 15 reps, with your hands on the paddle for added stability
- Planks: 3 sets of 1 minute each

Cool Down and Stretching Exercises

Cooling down and stretching are important parts of any workout, including SUP. After a strenuous paddle or workout, it's crucial to spend time cooling down and stretching to prevent injury, increase flexibility, and promote relaxation.

Here are some cool-down and stretching exercises that you can do after a SUP workout:

- **Seated Forward Fold:** Sit with your legs stretched out in front of you and reach forward to touch your toes or ankles.
- **Shoulder Rolls:** Roll your shoulders in a circular motion, first forward and then backward.
- **Cat-Cow Stretch:** Get into a tabletop position with your hands and knees on the board. Inhale and arch your back to stretch your spine, then exhale and

round your back to stretch your abs.

- **Figure Four Stretch:** Sit on the board with your legs crossed, and place your right ankle over your left knee. Gently press down on your right knee to stretch your hip.

- **Chest Opener:** Stand up and clasp your hands behind your back, lifting your arms away from your body to stretch your chest and shoulders.

Modifying for Different Fitness Levels

When it comes to SUP workouts, it's best to modify the routine based on your fitness level. Remember, everyone's fitness level is different, and it's important not to be too hard on yourself if you can't perform a workout.

A hack is to give yourself some time. And by then, you'll build strength and stamina. You'll also be strong enough to tackle more challenging workouts.

Here are some tips on how to do just that:

- **Adjust the intensity:** If you're a beginner and you haven't tried SUP workouts before, you may need to start with less intense exercises and shorter intervals. Just increase the intensity and duration gradually as you build strength and stamina.

- **Modify the exercises:** If an exercise is too challenging, try a modification. For example, if push-ups on the paddleboard are too difficult for you, don't insist on doing them. Instead, try doing them on your knees instead.

- **Use lighter weights:** If you're using a paddle as a weight, start with a lighter paddle or use no weight at all. As you get stronger, you can gradually increase the weight of the paddle.

- **Take breaks:** Don't be afraid to take breaks during

the workout, especially if you feel fatigued or out of breath. It's better to take a break and continue than to push yourself too hard and risk injury.

- **Listen to your body:** Always listen to your body and stop exercising if you feel any pain or discomfort. It's better to err on the side of caution and rest rather than pushing yourself too hard and getting injured.

SUP Yoga and Workout Classes and Retreats

Attending a SUP yoga and workout class or retreat can provide professional guidance, variety in workout routines, group support, and the opportunity to exercise in scenic locations. With the guidance of a trained instructor, you can safely and effectively challenge yourself while avoiding injury.

Group support can help you stay accountable to your fitness goals, and the variety of workout routines can prevent boredom. Plus, the opportunity to exercise in scenic locations can add a fun and unique element to your fitness routine.

What to Expect

When showing up to a SUP yoga and workout class or retreat, you can expect a unique and challenging workout experience that combines the benefits of yoga and fitness with the natural beauty of being on the water.

Here are some things you can expect:

- **A combination of yoga and fitness exercises:** SUP yoga and workout classes typically include a

mix of yoga poses and fitness exercises, such as squats and lunges, to provide a full-body workout.
- **Modifications for all levels:** The instructor will typically provide modifications for different skill levels so that everyone in the class can participate and feel challenged.
- **A welcoming and supportive environment:** SUP yoga and workout classes and retreats are typically held in a relaxed and fun environment, where participants can enjoy the natural surroundings and support each other in their fitness journey.
- **A focus on mindfulness:** In addition to the physical benefits of the workout, there's typically a focus on mindfulness and relaxation, which can help reduce stress and promote overall well-being.

Recommendations

Interested in trying a SUP yoga and workout class or retreat?

Don't rush and sign up for the first offer. The goal is to join a near-perfect class and have an unforgettable experience.

Here are some recommendations for finding one that's right for you:

- **Research online:** Start by researching SUP yoga and workout classes or retreats online. Look for reviews and recommendations from other participants.
- **Ask for referrals:** Ask friends or family members who have attended yoga and workout classes or retreats for referrals.
- **Check with local gyms or yoga studios:** Check with local gyms or yoga studios to see if they offer

SUP yoga and workout classes or if they can recommend any.

- **Look for certified instructors:** Make sure the instructors leading the class or retreat are certified by a reputable organization, such as Yoga Alliance or the World Paddle Association.
- **Consider your skill level:** Look for a class or retreat that matches your skill level. If you're a beginner, look for classes that are specifically designed for beginners.
- **Check the location:** Make sure the location of the class or retreat is convenient for you and that it's in a scenic location that you'll enjoy.
- **Confirm equipment provided:** Make sure the class or retreat provides all the necessary equipment, such as paddleboards and paddles or find out if you need to bring your own.

SUP in Retirement Homes

SUP is an excellent low-impact exercise that can improve balance, strength, and flexibility. It is also a fun way to get a workout while enjoying the water. As SUP can be done in a swimming pool, it is a good activity for seniors who may have mobility issues or are not comfortable in open water.

According to research, retirement homes that offer SUP activities typically provide participants with a paddleboard, paddle, and personal flotation device. The activities are usually led by trained instructors who provide guidance and support to ensure the safety and comfort of the seniors (*Why Stand Up Paddleboarding Is Perfect for Seniors*, 2023).

Other than the physical benefits, SUP activities in retirement homes also provide an opportunity for socialization and community building among the residents.

Participants can enjoy the company of their peers while engaging in a fun and healthy activity.

If you or someone you know is living in a retirement home, consider inquiring about SUP activities as part of the exercise program. It is a great way to stay active, healthy, and social in a safe and comfortable environment.

Apart from the benefits mentioned above, here are the other perks of SUP activities:

- **Mental health benefits:** SUP provides an opportunity to enjoy nature and get outdoors, which can have positive effects on mental health and well-being, particularly for seniors who may experience social isolation or depression.

- **Fun and social:** SUP can be a fun and social activity, allowing seniors to connect with others and enjoy a sense of community while getting exercise.

Fun Fact

Did you know SUP yoga provides an extra challenge to traditional yoga practice, as the instability of the water adds a new dimension to the poses?

Practicing yoga on a SUP board can improve balance, strength, and focus, and it offers a unique and serene experience of being surrounded by water and nature.

Chapter 8: Travel Tips

Imagine floating on crystal clear waters, surrounded by stunning scenery, and feeling the sun's warmth on your skin. You can make this dream a reality by traveling with your SUP board to some of the most breathtaking destinations in the world.

Whether you're planning a tropical escape, an adventure in the mountains, or a coastal road trip, bringing your SUP board along can add an exciting new element to your travels. However, before you pack your bags and board, there are a few things you should know to make the most out of your journey.

In this chapter, I'll give you a walkthrough of what you need to know about traveling with a SUP board and discuss the other option which is using a rental board later if you cannot bring your board with you.

Let's begin.

The Benefits of Traveling With a SUP Board

Travelling with a SUP board can offer numerous benefits that make it a kickass way to explore new destinations.

Here are some of the benefits of traveling with a SUP board:

- **Experience the beauty of nature:** One of the primary benefits of traveling with a SUP board is the opportunity to experience the beauty of nature in a unique way. Paddling along the coastline or exploring hidden coves and lagoons can give you a chance to see marine life up close and appreciate the natural beauty of your surroundings.

- **Get a workout:** SUP boarding is an excellent full-body workout that can help you stay fit and active while on vacation. Paddling works your core, arms, and legs, and can help you burn calories while enjoying the scenery.
- **Enjoy new adventures:** Traveling with a SUP board allows you to explore new destinations and embark on unique adventures. You can paddle through calm waters, ride waves, or even take a SUP yoga class.
- **Relieve stress:** SUP can be a relaxing activity that can help reduce stress levels. The sound of water and the gentle motion of paddling can have a calming effect, helping you unwind and recharge.
- **Connect with others:** SUP is a social activity that can help you connect with others. Whether you join a group paddle or rent boards with friends, it can be a fun way to make new connections and enjoy time with loved ones.
- **Explore new cultures:** SUP boarding can be a great way to explore new cultures and traditions. Many destinations have unique paddleboarding experiences that can offer insight into the local way of life.

Fun Fact

Did you know that you can actually take your SUP board on a plane as a checked baggage?

According to an article about inflatable paddleboards, some airlines allow a SUP board to be checked in as a piece of sporting equipment, just like a surfboard (Kidd, 2022). So, if you're planning to travel to a destination with great paddling spots, check if you can bring your paddleboard along for the adventure!

Research Your Destination

Researching your destination is an important step to take before traveling with a SUP board.

A cool way to put it is like the need to chart a course before setting sail on a journey. Just as a sailor would map out their journey, take note of hazards, and plan their route to ensure a safe and successful voyage, a paddler should also do their due diligence before venturing onto new waters with a SUP board.

Checking Regulations and Restrictions

Respecting local rules and regulations is essential when paddleboarding in a new location. Each area may have specific laws and guidelines that are in place to ensure the safety of all individuals and protect the environment.

Before heading out on the water, do some research to determine what local rules and regulations may apply. This could include rules about where to launch your board and areas to avoid.

By following local rules and regulations, you not only stay safe, but you also help to protect the environment and preserve the natural beauty of the area. This means leaving no trace, properly disposing of any waste, and avoiding any activities that may damage the surrounding ecosystem.

When traveling with a SUP board, research and check the regulations and restrictions of your destination. Of course, you don't want to get into trouble, do you?

Here's why you should always check the regulations and restrictions in your destination:

- **Compliance with local laws:** Different countries, states, and even municipalities may have specific rules and regulations regarding the use of SUP boards.

  For instance, some areas may require a permit to paddle in certain waterways, while others may prohibit SUP altogether. By checking these regulations before you go, you can ensure that you comply with local laws and avoid any legal issues.

- **Safety concerns:** Regulations and restrictions are often put in place to ensure the safety of both paddlers and other water users.

  Some waterways may have strong currents, dangerous wildlife, or other hazards that require special precautions. By researching and adhering to these regulations, you can minimize the risk of accidents or injuries.

- **Environmental protection:** Regulations and restrictions are also implemented to protect the environment and local wildlife.

  For instance, some areas may prohibit paddling in sensitive ecosystems, such as coral reefs or wetlands, to prevent damage to the ecosystem.

  Other areas may require you to follow certain guidelines, such as avoiding disturbing wildlife. By respecting these regulations, you can help preserve the natural beauty of the area for future generations.

Finding the Best SUP Spots

According to Johanson (2022), the perfect SUP spot depends on personal preferences and skill level. Yes, there are a few factors to consider, but what you consider "the perfect SUP spot" is up to you.

A good SUP spot should have calm and relatively flat water conditions, making it easy to balance and paddle. It should also have clear water with good visibility, allowing you to see any obstacles or hazards.

The ideal SUP spot should offer a beautiful and scenic environment with stunning views, such as crystal-clear lakes, pristine rivers, or breathtaking coastlines. It should also have easy access to the water with ample parking and launch points.

Plus, the perfect SUP spot should offer a sense of adventure, whether it's exploring hidden coves, discovering wildlife, or catching some waves. Overall, a perfect SUP spot should provide a serene and enjoyable experience, allowing you to connect with nature and enjoy the therapeutic benefits of SUP.

Here are tips to help you find the best SUP spots:

- **Research online:** Start by researching online to find information about potential SUP spots. Look for articles, blogs, and forums that provide insights into the best locations for paddleboarding.

  You can also use online maps to locate waterways and find areas that are suitable for paddling.

- **Talk to locals:** Talking to locals can be a great way to find the best SUP spots in the area. They can provide insider tips and recommendations about hidden gems or popular spots that offer unique experiences.

- **Check weather and tides:** Check the weather and tides before you head out to ensure the conditions are suitable. Calm and clear weather conditions are ideal for SUP, and it's best to avoid windy or stormy days.

- **Join a SUP community:** Joining a SUP community is an excellent way to connect with other paddlers and find the best SUP spots. They can provide valuable insights into their favorite spots and offer tips on the best times to paddle.

- **Use local guides or instructors:** Local guides or instructors can offer valuable information about the best SUP spots in the area. They can also provide lessons and tours, allowing you to discover new locations and learn new skills.

Additionally, they can offer insights into the local history, culture, and environment, making your paddling experience more enriching and enjoyable.

Learning Local Weather and Water Conditions

Familiarizing yourself with local weather and water conditions is an essential aspect of planning a successful SUP trip.

Here are some reasons why:

- **Safety:** Understanding local weather and water conditions is critical to ensure your safety while paddleboarding.

For example, strong currents can make it difficult to paddle, and cold water temperatures can cause hypothermia.

Knowing the local weather conditions and water temperatures can help you prepare appropriately, such as bringing the right gear and dressing in appropriate layers.

- **Paddling efficiency:** Understanding local weather and water conditions can help you plan your route and optimize your paddling efficiency.

For example, wind direction and strength can affect your speed and direction, so it's essential to plan your route accordingly.

- **Overall experience:** Understanding local weather and water conditions can enhance your overall paddling experience.

  By being aware of the local conditions, you can choose the best time and location to paddle, ensuring an enjoyable and memorable experience.

Travel with your board

It would be great if you can take your own SUP board on vacation with you and it can lead to an unforgettable SUP session. Your experience will not only be worth your while but also allow you to discover a new appreciation for paddleboarding in more locations.

However if you have a large hard board and want to travel by air, it can be challenging or not even possible.

I took my SUP board with me when travelling by air but had to book my flights with a certain airline. So it can be feasible if your board meets the airline's oversized check-in baggage or sports equipment regulations. Check with your airline if you are not sure. Also, make sure you have a way to transport your board once you arrive at your destination. If you want to use a rent-a-car, I recommend you to bring your soft roof rack with you so that you can put your board on the car.

If you want to travel by car with your hard board, you just need a roof rack, straps, and travel bag as an option. Or if you want to take your inflatable SUP board, then you can just pack and go.

If you do not have any option to bring your board on vacation, you can use a rental board at your destination if available. It can be a good experience to try a different board.

Choosing an Inflatable Board

Here are some factors to consider when choosing an inflatable board for travel:

- **Portability:** When traveling, it's important to choose a board that is easy to transport. Consider the weight and size of the SUP board when deflated.

  A lightweight and compact board can easily fit into a backpack or luggage.

- **Durability:** Your SUP board will be exposed to different environments and conditions during travel, so it's important to choose a durable board that can withstand wear and tear.

  Look for boards made with strong materials such as PVC or drop-stitch construction.

- **Stability:** Depending on where you plan to paddle, you may need a more stable board. If you plan to paddle in choppy waters or surf, a wider and more stable board will be more appropriate.

  However, if you plan to paddle in calm waters, you can choose a narrower board for a faster and more maneuverable experience.

- **Inflation time:** Some SUP boards take longer to inflate than others, which can be a hassle when you're on the go. Consider the inflation time of the board and whether you have access to a power source or pump when traveling.

- **Accessories:** Look for SUP boards that come with essential accessories such as a travel paddle, fin, and carrying bag.

  Some boards also come with extra features such as bungee cords for gear storage, built-in handles, and D-rings for attaching a leash.

- **Budget:** The price of a paddleboard can vary widely depending on the brand, size, and features. Set a budget and look for a board that fits within your price range without compromising on quality

Protecting Your Board and Paddle

Protecting your SUP board and paddle during travel ensures that they remain in good condition and can be used during your trip. When traveling with your board, invest in a high-quality board bag that provides ample padding and protection from bumps and scratches. You may also want to bring a travel paddle that comes apart into two or three pieces.

Also, if you are bringing an inflatable board, ensure you pack your board correctly, including deflating and rolling it up tightly to minimize the risk of damage during transport. Proper protection and handling of your board during travel can save you from costly repairs or having to replace your board altogether.

A Board Bag

Inflatable boards come with board bags. In most cases, those bags are enough.

However, matters are different when you're traveling with hard boards. Traveling with hard boards requires extra precautions to ensure that they are protected from damage during transport.

If you'll be traveling with a hard board, one of the most important things you can do to ensure its safe arrival is to use a travel bag which has a protective layer guarding your SUP board against scratches, dings, and other damages that may happen during transportation.

When choosing a board bag, consider the level of protection that suits your needs.

Board bags for daily use, for example, provide a basic level of protection from minor scratches and dings. Meanwhile, padded bags or travel bags offer more robust protection against impacts and rough handling.

Here are some tips for choosing and using a board bag for your SUP board:

- **Guarantee a good fit:** Measure your board carefully to ensure you get the right size bag. A snug fit will prevent your board from shifting around during transit and potentially causing damage.

- **Prioritize durability:** Choose a bag made from durable materials that can withstand the rigors of travel. Heavy-duty zippers and reinforced stitching are essential for a long-lasting protective layer.

- **Use a travel bag:** If you're traveling by plane, consider investing in a travel bag that meets airline regulations for oversized baggage. This will provide maximum protection for your board and reduce the risk of damage from baggage handlers.

- **Add an external layer:** Use foam padding or bubble wrap to provide extra protection for the most vulnerable areas of your board, such as the nose and tail. Secure these padding materials with tape to prevent them from slipping during transit.

- **Clean it up:** When packing your hard board into the bag, make sure it's clean and dry to avoid mold or mildew growth during storage. Remove the fins if possible and wrap them separately to prevent damage.

Proper Packing

Proper packing is essential to prevent damage to your SUP board during travel.

Here are some tips for packing your board to ensure it arrives at your destination in good condition:

- **Deflate your board (if it's inflatable):** Before packing your inflatable board, deflate it completely and remove any fins or accessories. This will make it easier to pack and reduce the risk of damage during transport.
- **Use a board bag (for a hard board):** As mentioned earlier, using a board bag is essential to protect your board during travel. Make sure your SUP board fits snugly inside the bag and is well-padded.
- **Wrap accessories separately:** If you are packing any accessories such as fins, paddles, or leashes, wrap them separately in bubble wrap or other protective materials to prevent them from scratching or damaging the board.
- **Place your fins and paddle blade in the center of your luggage:** If you are packing your accessories, place them in the center with clothing or other soft items packed around them for additional padding.
- **Label your luggage:** Make sure your board bag or luggage is clearly labeled with your name and contact information. This will help ensure that it is not lost or misplaced during travel.
- **Consider a travel bag:** If you are traveling by air and have a particularly expensive or fragile board, consider investing in a travel bag for extra protection.

Renting vs. Buying

If you don't have the space or resources to bring your own SUP board, renting one at your destination is a great option. Many rental companies can help you. Just make sure to check reviews and prices in advance.

Why Rent?

Renting a SUP board at your travel destination offers several advantages over purchasing one and bringing it with you. Firstly, transporting your own board can be cumbersome and expensive, especially when flying.

Renting also allows you to try out different board types and sizes without committing to purchasing expensive equipment. Rental companies often provide valuable local knowledge and advice on the best spots to paddle, ensuring you have a safe and enjoyable experience.

Renting can be more cost-effective if you only paddle occasionally or if you are traveling to a new location.

Here are some tips to keep in mind when renting a SUP board:

- **Research rental companies:** Before choosing a rental company, read reviews and check prices to ensure you are getting a fair deal. Look for a company with a good reputation for quality equipment and customer service.
- **Reserve in advance if possible:** During peak travel seasons, SUP board rentals can sell out quickly. Make sure to reserve your board in advance to ensure availability.
- **Ask about delivery and pickup services:** Some rental companies offer delivery and pickup services,

making it easier for you to get your board to and from the water.
- **Check equipment before renting:** Before renting a SUP board, inspect it for any damage or signs of wear and tear. Make sure the board is clean and in good condition before you take it out on the water.

Getting Rid of the Hassle

Traveling with a SUP board can be a hassle. Not only do you need to transport a large, cumbersome board, but you also need to worry about the added cost of baggage fees and potential damage to the board during transit.

Additionally, not all transportation modes, such as buses or trains, may be able to accommodate the size of the board.

Renting a SUP board at your travel destination eliminates these concerns, allowing you to avoid the hassle of traveling with your own board. You can still enjoy the experience of paddleboarding in a new location without the added stress and cost of transporting your equipment.

Dressing Appropriately

Dressing appropriately for the conditions and weather is crucial when paddleboarding. Water and weather conditions can change quickly and it's important to be prepared for any situation.

In colder water or weather conditions, wearing a wetsuit or dry suit can keep you warm and comfortable while on the water. It's also important to wear appropriate footwear, such as water shoes or booties, to protect your feet from rocks and other hazards or keep your feet warm.

In warmer water or weather conditions, lightweight, breathable clothing and a hat can help protect you from the sun and keep you cool. It's also important to wear a life jacket or PFD at all times while on the water, regardless of weather conditions, unless you are surfing or trying Yoga.

Using Wetsuits and Rash Guards

Wetsuits and rash guards are commonly used in SUP to provide protection and enhance comfort while on the water.

Wetsuits
Wetsuits are designed to keep the body warm in colder water conditions. Made of neoprene material, wetsuits trap a thin layer of water between the suit and the skin, which is then warmed by the body's heat. This layer of warm water helps to insulate the body from the cold water outside the suit.

Rash Guards
Rash guards are lightweight, quick-drying shirts that provide protection from the sun and prevent chafing or irritation from rubbing against the board or paddle. They are typically made of a stretchy, breathable material that allows for freedom of movement and comfort while on the water.

Both wetsuits and rash guards can enhance the paddleboarding experience by providing protection and comfort in different water and weather conditions.

The Usefulness of a PFD

PFD is short for Personal Floating Device.

Wearing a PFD is helpful when paddleboarding, as it can potentially save your life in the event of an emergency. Even the most experienced paddlers can be caught off guard by sudden weather changes, equipment failures, or other unforeseen circumstances.

A PFD is designed to keep you afloat and support your head and neck in the water, allowing you to conserve energy and stay alive until help arrives. It's important to wear a PFD that is properly fitted and appropriate for your weight and size. In some areas, it may also be required by law to wear a PFD while paddleboarding.

Wearing a PFD can also increase confidence and comfort while on the water. If you're yet to consider yourself as a seasoned paddler, it can grant you peace of mind. Knowing that you are properly equipped for any situation lets you focus on enjoying the paddleboarding experience.

Knowing Your Limits

While it may be tempting to push yourself to try new things or explore new areas, it's important to recognize your own skill level and limitations.

Start with basic techniques and gradually increase your skill level and stamina over time. It's also important to be aware of any medical conditions or physical limitations that may affect your ability to paddleboard.

Not knowing your limits can be a dangerous and potentially life-threatening situation. It's essential to understand your physical and mental capabilities to avoid harm to yourself and others.

Here are some possible dangers of not knowing your limits:

- **Physical injury:** Pushing yourself beyond your limits can result in physical injury. Overexertion, fatigue, and strain can lead to muscle damage, bone fractures, and other serious injuries.

    For example, if you're not used to intense physical activity and try to climb a mountain or go on a long hike, you could experience fatigue and physical strain, increasing your risk of injury.

- **Dehydration and heat exhaustion:** Not knowing your limits can also put you at risk for dehydration and heat exhaustion. If you're not used to hot and humid weather or intense physical activity, you may not recognize the signs of heat exhaustion or dehydration until it's too late.

  Symptoms include dizziness, confusion, nausea, and rapid heartbeat, which can lead to more severe conditions such as heat stroke.

- **Hypothermia:** Similarly, not knowing your limits in cold weather can result in hypothermia. If you're not properly dressed or prepared for the weather conditions, you may be at risk of hypothermia, a condition where your body temperature drops dangerously low.

  Symptoms include shivering, confusion, and lethargy, which can lead to loss of consciousness and even death.

- **Dangerous behavior:** Not knowing your limits can result in dangerous behavior, such as excessive risk-taking. While wanting to "walk the extra mile" can be satisfying, it can also jeopardize your safety. Worse, if you're not aware of your limits and boundaries, you may engage in activities that put other people in danger.

Avoiding Unnecessary Risks

Avoiding unnecessary risks is key to a safe and enjoyable SUP experience. It's important to assess the water and weather conditions, as well as your own skill level and limitations, before setting out on the water.

Some common examples of unnecessary risks in SUP include:

- **Paddling in dangerous or unknown waters:** It's important to research and assess the water and weather conditions before paddling and to avoid areas that pose unnecessary risks, such as strong currents or dangerous wildlife.

- **Ignoring safety guidelines and regulations:** This includes not wearing a PFD or other safety equipment, paddling in restricted areas, or disregarding local laws and regulations.

- **Overestimating your own abilities:** It's important to recognize your own skill level and physical limitations and avoid attempting maneuvers or conditions that are beyond your ability.

- **Failing to plan ahead:** This includes not checking the weather forecast or not bringing appropriate safety equipment or supplies.

Conclusion

SUP has earned its place in the hearts of so many people worldwide. This is because of its unique combination of physical exercise, relaxation, and adventure. It's no surprise that it has gained so much popularity, as it's an experience that can be enjoyed by people of all ages and skill levels.

Whether you're a seasoned pro or a curious beginner, this book provides an extensive guide to SUP that covers everything you need to know to get started or explore your SUP options.

The book is divided into eight chapters, each focusing on a specific aspect of SUP.

Recap:

- **Chapter 1**

    The first chapter of this book serves as an introduction to stand-up paddleboarding (SUP) and covers the different types of waterways that are suitable for the activity.

    From calm lakes to rushing rivers, to vast oceans, and even canals and swamps, this chapter explores the various SUP environments and offers insights into the fishing aspect of SUP.

    Additionally, readers will discover tips on how to become a SUP angler and learn about the exciting sport of SUP fishing.

- **Chapter 2**

    The second chapter of this book is all about the essential equipment needed for SUP. It covers the different types of boards, paddles, leashes, and carriers that are required for an enjoyable SUP adventure.

This chapter offers helpful tips on how to choose the right board that suits your skill level, preferences, and the type of waterway you plan to explore. It also includes information on board materials, repair, and other gear needed for a successful SUP experience.

- **Chapter 3**

  The third chapter of this book is dedicated to gear, safety measures, and basic skills that are essential for a successful SUP adventure. It covers the necessary equipment and accessories that are useful during a SUP session, including life jackets, waterproof bags, and more.

  This chapter also offers valuable tips on dressing appropriately and following local rules and regulations to ensure a safe and enjoyable experience. Additionally, readers will discover the super basic skills required for SUP, such as proper paddling technique and balance.

- **Chapter 4**

  The fourth chapter of this book explores the various techniques for achieving speed in SUP, including downwind, race, and rapids (whitewater) techniques. Readers will learn about unforgettable downwind races in history, how to race in the river, how to paddle through rapids in the river, and more.

  This chapter also offers inspiration and motivation for those looking to take their SUP skills to the next level and achieve greater speed and control on the water.

- **Chapter 5**

  The fifth chapter of this book is all about surfing techniques for SUP, including how to paddle out, catch a wave in surf stance, and follow proper surf etiquette. Readers will also learn about the importance of surf forecasts, tides, and conditions when planning a SUP surfing session.

With this chapter, readers will gain a solid foundation in SUP surfing techniques and knowledge, which will help them get the most out of their time on the water.

- **Chapter 6**

  The sixth chapter of the book explores SUP foil techniques, including pumping, carving, and downwind foiling. It delves into the impact of foiling on the SUP community and how it has revolutionized the sport.

  The chapter also shares thoughts from the surfing community and how foiling has changed the lineup. The future of SUP foil looks bright, and this chapter offers insights into this exciting aspect of SUP.

- **Chapter 7**

  The seventh chapter of the book is dedicated to SUP yoga and workout. It explains the benefits of SUP yoga and workout and the necessary equipment for them. It also provides beginner, intermediate, and advanced SUP yoga poses along with a SUP yoga sequence.

  The chapter also includes a SUP workout routine and tips for modifying it for different fitness levels. Finally, it covers SUP yoga and workout classes and retreats, what to expect, and recommendations.

- **Chapter 8**

  The last chapter of the book provides valuable travel tips for SUP enthusiasts. It covers essential considerations like researching your destination, choosing the right board for travel, dressing appropriately, and following local rules and regulations.

It also includes tips on packing and transporting your gear and what to expect when traveling with your board. Whether you are a seasoned traveler or a first-time adventurer, this chapter will equip you with the knowledge you need to plan a successful and memorable SUP trip.

Put them all together, and you'll realize that this book provides a comprehensive guide to SUP that covers everything from the basics to advanced techniques. It's an excellent resource for you—and anyone looking to get started with SUP, have the right equipment, or hone their skills.

With SUP, the world is your oyster. And with this book as your guide, you can confidently explore new waterways, enjoy the thrill of downwind racing, catch waves for fun or like a professional, and even combine SUP with yoga and workouts.

So grab your board, paddle, and safety gear, and let's dive into the exciting world of stand-up paddleboarding!

If you enjoyed the book, please leave a review on Amazon.

References

Burns, C. (2022, April 25). *How Many Calories Does Stand Up Paddle Boarding Burn*? Paddle Board Gear. https://paddleboardgear.net/sup-fitness/how-many-calories-does-stand-up-paddle-boarding-burn/

Caranto, T. (2022, July 10). *How To Position A Fin On A SUP: SUP Tips*. Supconnect.com. https://www.supconnect.com/tips/how-to-position-a-fin-on-a-sup

Carolina Cup | Wrightsville Beach, NC 28480. (n.d.). Wilmington and Beaches. https://www.wilmingtonandbeaches.com/event/carolina-cup/4603/

Closier, G. (2020, March 13). *Downwind Foil: a Step-by-Step Guide*. TotalWing. https://www.totalwing.com/news/how-to-downwind-foil-greg-closier/

Cox, A. (2023, January 29). *SUP Fitness: How Many Calories Does Paddle Boarding Burn?* Supconnect. https://www.supconnect.com/tips/sup-fitness-how-many-calories-does-paddle-boarding-burn

De Haan, D. (2020, May 26). *25 SUP Board Tips - How To Paddle Board Like A Pro Today - Stand Up Paddle Boards Review*. Stand up Paddleboards Review. https://www.standuppaddleboardsreview.com/sup-board-tips/

Felicity, T. (2022, July 2). *Tips for Choosing the Best Stand Up Paddle Board*. Tech Times. https://www.techtimes.com/articles/277273/20220702/tips-for-choosing-the-best-stand-up-paddle-board.htm

Gorge Paddle Challenge 2022 - Hood River. (n.d.). Local Freshies. https://localfreshies.com/event/gorge-paddle-challenge-hood-river

Johanson, M. (2022, February 7). *9 best places for stand-up paddleboarding (SUP) adventures*. Lonely Planet. https://www.lonelyplanet.com/articles/best-destinations-long-distance-sup-adventures

Kidd, J. (2022, October 14). *Can You Take an Inflatable Paddle Board on an Airplane?* Green Water Sports. https://greenwatersports.com/57485/can-you-take-an-inflatable-paddle-board-on-an-airplane

McCaw, P. (2022, October 12). *How to Fish From a Paddle Board: A Beginners Guide to SUP Fishing*. GILI Sports. https://www.gilisports.com/blogs/sup-fishing/how-to-fish-from-a-paddle-board

Nuttall, G. (2022, May 29). *Fishing From A Stand-Up Paddleboard: A Great Experience*. North American Deer Hunter. https://nadeerhunter.com/fishing-from-a-stand-up-paddleboard-a-great-experience/

Paddle Board world records to beat | Aquaplanet Sport. (n.d.). Aquaplanet. https://www.aquaplanetsports.com/blog/2022/09/26/paddle-boarding-world-records-could-you-do-better/

Perez, J. (n.d.). *3 Simple Steps To Improve Your Technique*. Cascadia Board Co. Retrieved March 19, 2023, from https://www.cascadiaboardco.com/blogs/sup-tips-tricks/3-simple-steps-to-improve-your-paddle-board-technique

Regan, J. (2020, May 25). *Fishing Paddle Board vs Fishing Kayak: Which is better?* GILI Sports. https://www.gilisports.com/blogs/sup-fishing/paddle-board-fishing-vs-kayak-fishing

Regan, J. (2021, March 11). *Ocean vs Lake Paddle Boarding: The Ultimate Guide.* GILI Sports. https://www.gilisports.com/blogs/sup-expert-advice/ocean-vs-lake-paddle-boarding

Roberts, E. (2022, September 1). *The 10 Very Best Stand-up Paddleboards.* The Strategist. https://nymag.com/strategist/article/best-stand-up-paddle-boards.html

Stinchcombe, C. (2022, July 27). *Go for a Float: A Beginner's Guide to Stand-Up Paddling.* The New York Times. https://www.nytimes.com/2022/07/27/well/move/stand-up-paddleboarding.html

Tilton, M. M. & M. (2022, August 18). *The Best Standup Paddleboards of 2022.* GearJunkie. https://gearjunkie.com/boats-water/sup/best-stand-up-paddle-board-sup

Top 5 SUP Events In the World - Paddle Boarding Race. (n.d.). Goosehill. https://goosehillsport.com/blogs/news/top-5-sup-events-in-the-world

12 Safety Tips for Safe Stand Up Paddle Boarding. (2022, September 1). Www.academyofsurfing.com. https://www.academyofsurfing.com/news/12-safety-tips-for-safe-stand-up-paddle-boarding

2022 — Molokai Holokai Maui to Molokai Challenge 2022 - Molokai Holokai Ho'olaulea Day 1 —. (n.d.). Raceroster.com. https://raceroster.com/events/2022/59513/molokai-holokai-maui-to-molokai-challenge-2022-molokai-holokai-hoolaulea-day-1

W, S. (n.d.). *What are Paddle Boards Made of? (SUP Construction).* Paddle Camp. https://paddlecamp.com/what-are-paddle-boards-made-of/

What Is Surf Culture In 2022? (2022, February 7). Www.academyofsurfing.com. https://www.academyofsurfing.com/news/what-is-surf-culture-in-2022

Why Stand Up Paddleboarding is Perfect for Seniors. (2023, February 10). Sea Gods. https://seagods.ca/blogs/articles/why-stand-up-paddleboarding-is-perfect-for-seniors

Made in the USA
Middletown, DE
21 May 2023